GOD

JOY

IN YOUR

HEART

CHARLES SPURGEON

WHITAKER
HOUSE

All Scripture quotations are taken from the King James Version (KJV) of the Holy Bible.

Editor's note: This book has been edited for the modern reader. Words, expressions, and sentence structure have been updated for clarity and readability.

God's Joy in Your Heart
(previously published as *Words of Cheer* and *Joy in Your Life*)

ISBN: 978-1-64123-958-5
eBook ISBN: 978-1-64123-959-2
Printed in Colombia
© 1998 by Whitaker House

Whitaker House
30 Hunt Valley Circle
New Kensington, PA 15068
web site: www.whitakerhouse.com

Library of Congress Cataloging-in-Publication Data

Spurgeon, C. H. (Charles Haddon), 1834–1892.
 [God's joy in your heart]
 Joy in your life / Charles Haddon Spurgeon.
    p. cm.
Originally published: God's joy in your heart. New Kensington, PA:
Whitaker House, ©1998.
 ISBN 0-88368-763-1
 1. Consolation. 2. Christian life—Baptist authors. I. Title.
 BV4905.3 .S69 2002
 242—dc21
                          2002004940

1 2 3 4 5 6 7 8 9 10 11 ⨂ 30 29 28 27 26 25 24 23

CONTENTS

ONE

SONS OF JACOB

For I am the Lord, I change not;
therefore ye sons of Jacob are not consumed.
—Malachi 3:6

The phrase *"sons of Jacob"* means persons who enjoy particular rights and titles. Jacob had no rights by birth, but he soon acquired them. He exchanged a mess of pottage with his brother Esau and thus gained the birthright. I do not justify the means, but he also obtained the blessing and so acquired unique rights.

"Sons of Jacob" also includes Christians who have unusual rights and titles, too. Unto those who believe, the Lord has given the right and power to become sons of God. They have an interest in the blood of Christ. They have a right to enter in through the gates into the city. They have a title to eternal honors. They have a promise of everlasting glory. They have a right to call

themselves sons of God. Yes, there are unique rights and privileges belonging to the *"sons of Jacob."*

But these *"sons of Jacob"* were men of unusual manifestations. Jacob had experienced unusual manifestations from his God, and thus he was highly honored. Once, at night, he lay down and slept. He had the hedges for his curtains, the sky for his canopy, a stone for his pillow, and the earth for his bed. Then he had an extraordinary manifestation. He saw angels of God ascending and descending a ladder from heaven to earth. He thus had a manifestation of Christ Jesus, as the ladder that reaches from earth to heaven, by which angels came up and down to bring us mercies.

And then, what a manifestation there was at Mahanaim, when the angels of God met Jacob! Again at Peniel, when Jacob wrestled with God, he saw Him face to face. Those were all unique, unusual manifestations. This passage refers to those who, like Jacob, have had remarkable manifestations.

The *"sons of Jacob"* have had unusual manifestations. They have talked with God as a man talks with his friend. They have whispered in the ear of Jehovah. Christ has been with them to eat with them, and they with Christ. The Holy Spirit has shone into their souls with such a mighty radiance that they could not doubt about special manifestations. The *"sons of Jacob"* are the men who enjoy these manifestations.

Then, they are men of unusual trials. Oh, poor Jacob! I would not choose Jacob's lot even if I did not have the prospect of Jacob's blessing, for a hard lot his was. He had to run away from his father's house to Laban's. Then that surly old Laban cheated him all the years he was there—cheated him of his wife, cheated him in his wages, cheated him in his flocks, and cheated him all through the story. By and by, he had to run away from Laban, who pursued him and overtook him. Next came Esau with four hundred men to cut him up, root and branch. Then there was a season of prayer, after which he wrestled and had to go the rest of his life with his thigh out of joint. However, a little later, his dearly beloved Rachel died. His daughter Dinah was led astray, and his sons murdered the Shechemites. Then his favored dear Joseph was sold into Egypt, and a famine came. Reuben went up to his bed and polluted it, Judah committed incest with his own daughter-in-law, and all his sons became a plague to him. At last Benjamin was taken away and the old man, almost broken-hearted, cried, *"Joseph is not, and Simeon is not, and ye will take Benjamin away"* (Genesis 42:36). Never was a man more tried than Jacob, all because of the one sin of cheating his brother. All through his life, God chastised him.

I believe there are many who can sympathize with dear old Jacob. They have had to pass through trials very much like his. Well, cross-bearers! God says, *"For I am the LORD, I change not; therefore ye sons of Jacob are not consumed."* Poor tried souls! You are not consumed because of the unchanging nature of your God. Now do not start fretting and say with the self-conceit of misery, *"I am the man who hath seen affliction"* (Lamentations 3:1). The Man of Sorrows was afflicted more than you; Jesus was indeed a mourner. You only see the skirts of the garments of affliction. You never have had trials like His. You do not understand what troubles mean. You have hardly sipped the cup of trouble. You have only had a drop or two, but Jesus drank the dregs. *"Fear not,"* says God, *"I am the LORD, I change not; therefore ye sons of Jacob,"* men of unusual trials, *"are not consumed."*

YOU DO NOT UNDERSTAND
WHAT TROUBLES MEAN.
YOU HAVE HARDLY SIPPED THE
CUP OF TROUBLE. YOU HAVE ONLY
HAD A DROP OR TWO, BUT JESUS
DRANK THE DREGS.

Then, "*sons of Jacob*" are men of exceptional character. Though there were some things about Jacob's character that we cannot commend, there are traits that God commends. There was Jacob's faith, by which Jacob had his name written among the mighty worthies who did not obtain the promises on earth, but will possess them in heaven. Are you a person of faith, beloved? Do you know what it is to walk by faith, to live by faith, to get your temporary food by faith, to live on spiritual manna—all by faith? Is faith the rule of your life? If so, you are a "*son of Jacob.*"

Jacob was a man of prayer—a man who wrestled, groaned, and prayed. "Ah, you poor heathen, don't you pray?" "No!" you say, "I never thought of such a thing. For years I have not prayed." Well, I hope you may before you die. Live and die without prayer, and you will pray long enough when you get to hell.

I knew a woman who was so busy sending her children to Sunday school that she said she had no time to pray. No time to pray? Had she time to dress? There is a time for every purpose under heaven, and if she had purposed to pray, she would have prayed.

Sons of God cannot live without prayer. They are wrestling Jacobs. They are men in whom the Holy Spirit so works that they can no more live without prayer than I can live without breathing. They must pray. Mark you, if you are living without prayer, you are living without Christ; and, dying like that, your portion will be in the lake that burns with fire. May God redeem and rescue you from such a lot! But you who are "*the sons of Jacob*" take comfort, for God is immutable.

TWO

FAITH VERSUS FEAR

He will put strength in me.
—Job 23:6

When the believer is brought into peace with God, he does not tremble at the thought of God's power. He does not ask, "Will He plead against me with His great power?" But he says, "No, that very power, once my terror and fear, is now my refuge and my hope, for He will put that very power in me. I rejoice that God is Almighty, for He will lend me His omnipotence. *'He will put strength in me.'* The very power that would have damned my soul saves my soul. The very power that would have crushed me God puts into me, so that the work of salvation may be accomplished. No, He will not use it to crush me, but He will put that very strength into me."

Do you see the Mighty One upon His throne? "Dread Sovereign, I see Your ominous arm. What, will You crush this sinner? Will You utterly destroy me with Your strength?" "No," says He, "come here, child." If you do go to His almighty throne, He says, "There, the same arm that made you quake, see there, I give it to you. Go out and live. I have made you mighty as I am, to do My works. I will put strength into you. The same strength that would have broken you to pieces on the wheel will now be put into you, so that you may do mighty works."

Now, this great strength sometimes goes out in prayer. Did you ever hear the prayers of a man in whom God had put strength? I venture to say, you have heard some of us poor puny souls pray, but have you ever heard a man pray that God had made into a giant? Oh, if you have, you will say it is a mighty thing to hear such a man in supplication.

I have seen such a man as if he had seized the angel and would pull him down. I have seen him now and then slip in his wrestling. But, like a giant, he has recovered his footing and seemed, like Jacob, to hurl the angel to the ground. I have marked the man lay hold of the throne of mercy and declare, "*Lord, I will not let you go, except you bless me*" (Genesis 32:26). I have seen him, when heaven's gates have been apparently barred, go up to them and say, "Gates, open wide in Jesus' name." Then I have seen the gates fly open before the man as if he were God himself, for he is armed with God Almighty's strength. I have seen that man discover in prayer some great mountain in his way and pray it down until it became a tiny molehill. He has beaten the hills and made them like chaff by the immensity of his might in prayer.

Some of you think I am talking enthusiasm, but such cases have there been and are now. Oh, to have heard Luther pray! When Melanchthon was dying, Luther went to his death-bed and said, "Melanchthon, you must not die!" "Oh," said Melanchthon, "I must die! It is a world of such toil and trouble." Luther said, "I have need of you, and God's cause has need of you, and as my name is Luther, you shall not die!" The physician said he would.

Well, down went Luther on his knees and began to tug at death. Old Death struggled mightily for Melanchthon, and he had got him well-nigh on his shoulders. "Drop him," said Luther, "I want him." Death replied, "No, he is my prey. I will take him!" "Down with him," commanded Luther, "Down with him, Death, or I will wrestle with you!" And he seemed to take hold of the grim monster and hurl him to the ground. Luther came away victorious, like Orpheus with his wife, up from the very shades of death. He had delivered Melanchthon from death by prayer!

"Oh," you say, "that is an extraordinary case." No, not one-half as extraordinary as you dream. Men and women have done the same in other cases. They have asked something of God and have been granted it. They have been to the throne, showed a promise, said they would not come away without its fulfillment, and have come back from God's throne conquerors of the Almighty, for prayer moves the arm that moves the world. "Prayer is the sinew of God," said one, "It moves His arm." And so it is. Truly, in prayer, with the strength of the faithful heart, there is a beautiful fulfillment of the text, *"He will put strength in me."*

Not only in prayer, but in duty, the man who has great faith in God, and whom God has girded with strength, becomes gigantic! Have you never read of those great heroes who put to flight whole armies and scattered kings like seed that is sown broadcast? Have you never read of those men who were fearless of foes and stalked onward before all their opposers, as if they would as soon die as live?

I read of a case in the old kirk of Scotland that occurred before King James, who wished to force "the black prelacy" on them. Andrew Melville and some of his associates were deputized to wait upon the king. As they were going with a scroll already written, they were warned to take care and return, for their lives were at stake. They paused a moment, and Andrew said, "I am not afraid, thank God, nor feeble-spirited in the cause and message of Christ. Come what pleases God to send us, our commission will be executed." At these words the delegation took courage and went forward.

On reaching the palace and having obtained an audience, they found his majesty attended by Lennox, Arran, and several other lords, all of whom were English. They presented the scroll with their strong objections. Arran lifted it from the table and glanced over it. He then turned to the ministers and furiously demanded, "Who dares sign these treasonable articles?" "We dare," replied Andrew Melville, "and we will render our lives in the cause." Having thus spoken, he came forward to the table, took the pen, subscribed his name, and was followed by his brethren. Arran and Lennox were confounded. The king looked on in silence, and the nobles in surprise.

Thus did our good forefathers appear before kings, and yet were not ashamed. "*The proud have had* [them] *greatly in derision, yet have* [they] *not declined from thy law"* (Psalm 119:51). Having thus discharged their duty, after a brief conference, the ministers were permitted to depart in peace. The king trembled more at them than if a whole army had been at his gates. Why was this? It was because God had put His own strength into them to make them masters of their duty.

You have some such in your midst now. Despised they may be, but God has made them like the lionly men of David, who would go down into the pit in the depths of winter, take the lion by the throat, and slay him. We have some in our churches—a remnant, I admit—who are not afraid to serve their God, like Abdiel, who was *"found faithful"* (1 Corinthians 4:2) among the faithless. We have some who are superior to the customs of the age and scorn to bow at mammon's knee, who will not use the trim language of too many modern ministers, but stand out for God's Gospel and the pure white banner of Christ, unstained and unsullied by the doctrines of men. Then are they mighty! Why they are mighty is because God has put strength in them.

"And will I be able to hold on to the end?" says the believer. Yes, you will, for God's strength is in you. "Will I be able to bear such a trial?" Yes, you will. Cannot Omnipotence stem the torrent? Omnipotence is in you. Like Ignatius of old, you are a God-bearer. You bear God about within you. Your heart is a temple of the Holy Spirit, and you will yet overcome.

"But can I ever stand firm in such an evil day?" Oh, yes you will, for He will put His strength in you!

Some time ago, I was in the company of some other ministers. One of them observed, "Brother, if there were to be stakes in Smithfield again, I am afraid they would find very few to

LIKE IGNATIUS OF OLD, YOU ARE
A GOD-BEARER. YOU BEAR GOD
ABOUT WITHIN YOU. YOUR HEART
IS A TEMPLE OF THE HOLY SPIRIT,
AND YOU WILL YET OVERCOME.

burn among us." "Well," I said, "I do not know anything about how you would burn. But this I know very well, that there never will be any lack of men who are ready to die for Christ." "Oh!" said he, "But they are not the right sort of men." "Well," said I, "but do you think they are the Lord's children?" "Yes, I believe they are, but they are not the right sort." "Ah," said I, "you would find them the right sort, if they came to the test, every one of them. They do not have burning grace yet. What would be the use of it? We do not need the grace until the stakes come, but we should have burning grace in burning moments."

If now a hundred of us were called to die for Christ, I believe there would not only be found a hundred, but five hundred, that would march to death and sing all the way. Whenever I find faith, I believe God will put strength into the man. I never think anything to be impossible to a man with faith in God, while it is written, *"He will put strength in me."*

Caesar could not swim the Tiber, encumbered as he was. Do you hope to swim the Jordan with your flesh about you? No, you will sink unless Jesus, as Aeneas carried Anchises upon his shoulders from the flames of Rome, would lift you from the Jordan and carry you across the stream. You will never be able to walk across the river or face that tyrant and smile in his face, unless you have something more than mortal flesh to depend on. You will need then to be belted about with the girdle of divinity, or else your loins will be loosed and your strength will fail you when you need it most. Many a man has ventured to the Jordan in his own strength, but how he has shrieked and howled when the first wave touched his feet! But no weakling ever went to death with God in him, except he found himself mightier than the grave. Go on, Christian, for this is your promise, *"He will put strength in me."*

> Weak, though I am,
> Yet through His might,
> I all things can perform.

Go on. Do not dread God's power, but rejoice in this: He will put His strength in you. He will not use His power to crush you.

THREE

LIBERTY FROM THE FEAR
OF DEATH

Where the Spirit of the Lord is, there is liberty.
—2 Corinthians 3:17

The true child of God serves his Master more than he ever did anyone else. As Erskine penned:

> Slight now His loving presence if they can;
> No, no; His conquering kindness leads the van.
> When everlasting love exerts the sway,
> They judge themselves most kindly bound to obey;
> Bound by redeeming love in stricter sense,
> Than ever Adam was in innocence.

"Where the Spirit of the Lord is, there is liberty" from the fear of death. O death, how many a sweet cup have you made bitter!

O death, how many a revel have you broken up! O death, how many a gluttonous banquet have you spoiled! O death, how many a sinful pleasure have you turned into pain! Take the telescope and look through the vista of a few years. What do you see? Grim death in the distance, grasping his scythe. He is ever coming. What is behind him? It depends upon your own character. If you are the sons of God, there is the palm branch. If you are not, you know what follows death—hell follows him. O death, your specter has haunted many a house where sin otherwise would have rioted. O death, your chilly hand has touched many a heart that was big with lust and made it start, frightened from its crime. Oh, how many are slaves to the fear of death!

Half the people in the world are afraid to die. There are some madmen who can march up to the cannon's mouth. There are some fools who rush with bloody hands before their Maker's tribunal. But most men fear to die.

Who is the man who does not fear to die? I will tell you—the man who is a believer. Fear to die? Thank God, I do not. The cholera may come again. I pray to God it will not, but if it does, it matters not to me. I will toil and visit the sick by night and by day until I drop. If it takes me, sudden death is sudden glory.

And so it is with the weakest saint. The prospect of dissolution does not make you tremble. Sometimes you fear, but more often you rejoice. You sit down and calmly think of dying. What is death? It is a low porch through which you stoop to enter heaven. What is life? It is a narrow screen that separates us from glory, and death kindly removes it!

I recollect a saying of a good old woman, who said, "Afraid to die, sir? I have dipped my foot in Jordan every morning before breakfast for the last fifty years, and do you think I am afraid to die now?" Die? Why, we die hundreds of times. We *die daily* (1 Corinthians 15:31). We die every morning; we die each night when we sleep; by faith we die. And so, dying will be old work when we come to it. We will say, "Ah, death, you and I have been old acquaintances. I have had you in my bedroom every night. I have talked with you each day. I have had the skull upon my dressing table. I have often thought of you. Death, you have come at last, but you are a welcome guest. You are an angel of light and the best friend I have had." Why dread death, since there is no fear of God's leaving you when you come to die?

Here I must tell you that anecdote of the good Welsh lady, who, when she lay dying, was visited by her minister. He said to her, "Sister, are you sinking?" She answered him not a word, but looked at him with an incredulous eye. He repeated the question, "Sister, are you sinking?" She looked at him again as if she could not believe that he would ask such a thing. At last, rising a little in bed, she said, "Sinking? Did you ever know a sinner to sink through a rock? If I had been standing on the sand, I might sink; but, thank God, I am on the Rock of Ages, and there is no sinking there."

How glorious to die! O angels, come! O cohorts of the Lord of Hosts, stretch your wide wings and lift us up from earth. O winged seraphim, bear us far above the reach of this inferior plane. But until you come, I'll sing:

Since Jesus is mine,
I'll not fear undressing,
But gladly put off these garments of clay.
To die in the Lord is a covenant blessing,

Since Jesus to glory,
Through death led the way.

There are two sides to propositions such as this. There are some glorious things that we are free to. Not only are we freed from sin in every sense, from the law, and from the fear of death, but we are free to something. *"Where the Spirit of the Lord is, there is liberty."* That liberty gives us certain rights and privileges.

We are free to heaven's charter. The Magna Carta of heaven is the Bible, and you are free to it. There is a choice passage: *"When thou passest through the waters, I will be with thee; and through the rivers, they shall not overflow thee"* (Isaiah 43:2). You are free to that. Here is another: *"Mountains shall depart, and the hills be removed; but my kindness shall not depart"* (Isaiah 54:10). You are free to that. Here is another: *"Having loved His own... He loved them unto the end"* (John 13:1). You are free to that. *"Where the Spirit of the Lord is, there is liberty."*

Here is a chapter touching election; you are free to that if you are elect. Here is another, speaking of the noncondemnation of the righteous and their justification; you are free to that.

You are free to all that is in the Bible. It is a never-failing treasure, filled with boundless stores of grace. It is the bank of heaven: you may draw from it as much as you please without hindrance or abatement. Bring nothing with you except faith. Bring as much faith as you can muster, and you are welcome to all that is in the Bible. There is not a promise, not a word in it, that is not yours. In the depths of tribulation, let it comfort you. Amid waves of distress, let it cheer you. When sorrows surround you, let it be your helper. This is your Father's love-token.

You are free to all that is
in the Bible. It is a
never-failing treasure,
filled with boundless stores
of grace. It is the bank of
heaven: you may draw from
it as much as you please
without hindrance or
abatement. Bring nothing
with you except faith.

Let it never be shut and covered with dust. You are free to it, so use your freedom.

Next, remember that you are free to the throne of grace. It is the privilege of Englishmen that they can always send a petition to Parliament. Likewise, it is the privilege of a believer that he can always send a petition to the throne of God. I am free to God's throne. If I want to talk to God tomorrow morning, I can. If tonight I wish to have conversation with my Master, I can go to Him. I have a right to go to His throne. It matters not how much I have sinned. I go and ask for pardon. It signifies nothing how poor I am. I go and plead His promise that He will provide all things that I need. I have a right to go to His throne at all times, in midnight's darkest hour or in the heat of midday. Wherever I am—if fate commands me to the utmost verge of the wide earth—I have still constant admission to His throne. Use that right, beloved. Use that right on behalf of others as well as yourself.

There is not one of you who lives up to his privileges. Many a gentleman will live beyond his income, spending more than he has coming in. But there is not a Christian who does so—I mean, who lives up to his spiritual income. Oh, you have an infinite income, an income of promises, an income of grace. No Christian ever lived up to his income. Some people say, "If I had more money, I would have a larger house and horses and a carriage and so on." Very well and good, but I wish Christians would do the same. I wish they would set up a larger house and do greater things for God, look happier and take those tears away from their eyes.

With such stores in the bank and so much in hand that God gives you, you have no right to be poor. Rejoice, rejoice! The Christian ought to live up to his income, not below it.

Turn, then, my soul unto your rest,
The ransom of your great High Priest
Hath set the captive free.
Trust to His efficacious blood,
Nor fear your banishment from God,
Since Jesus died for thee.

FOUR

SUFFERING
AND CONSOLATION

For as the sufferings of Christ abound in us,
so our consolation also aboundeth by Christ.
—2 Corinthians 1:5

Just *"as the sufferings of Christ abound in us, so our consolation also aboundeth by Christ."* Here is a blessed proportion. God always keeps a pair of scales; in one side He puts his people's trials, and in the other He puts their consolations. When the scale of trials is nearly empty, you will always find the scale of consolation in nearly the same condition. When the scale of trials is full, you will find the scale of consolation just as heavy.

"As the sufferings of Christ abound in us, so our consolation also aboundeth by Christ." This is a matter of pure experience. Oh, it is mysterious that, when the black clouds gather the most,

the light within us is always brightest! When the night lowers and the tempest is coming on, the heavenly captain is always closest to his crew. It is a blessed thing, when we are most cast down, that then it is we are most lifted up by the consolations of Christ.

Trials make more room for consolation. There is nothing that makes a man have a big heart like a great trial. I always find that little, miserable people, whose hearts are about the size of a grain of mustard seed, never have had much to try them. I have found that those people who have no sympathy for their fellows—who never weep for the sorrows of others—very seldom have had any woes of their own.

Great hearts can only be made by great troubles. The spade of trouble digs the reservoir of comfort deeper and makes more room for consolation. When God comes into our heart and finds it full, He begins to break away our comforts and to make it empty. Then there is more room for grace. The humbler a man is, the more comfort he will always have.

I recall walking with a plowman one day, a man who was deeply taught, although he was a plowman. (Really, some plowmen would make better preachers than many college gentlemen.) He said to me, "Depend upon it, if you or I ever get one inch above the ground, we will get just that inch too high." I believe it is true. The lower we lie, the nearer to the ground we are, the more our troubles humble us, and the more fit we are to receive comfort. God always gives us comfort when we are most fit for it. That is one reason why consolations increase in the same ratio as our trials.

Then trouble exercises our graces, and the very exercise of our graces tends to make us more comfortable and happy. Where showers fall most, there the grass is greenest. I suppose the fogs and mists of Ireland make it "the Emerald Isle." Wherever you find great fogs of trouble and mists of sorrow, you always find emerald-green hearts, full of the beautiful verdure of the comfort and love of God. Christian, do not say, "Where have the swallows gone? They are gone. They are dead." Wrong you are. They are not dead. They have skimmed the purple sea and gone to a far-off land, but they will be back again soon.

Child of God, do not say the flowers are dead. Do not say the winter has killed them and they are gone. Ah, no, though winter has coated them with the ermine of its snow, they will put up their heads again and will be alive very soon. Do not say, child of God, that the sun is quenched, because the cloud has hidden it. Oh, no, he is behind there, brewing summer for you. When he comes out again, he will have made the clouds fit to drop in April showers, all of them mothers of the sweet May flowers.

Above all, when your God hides His face, do not say that He has forgotten you. He is but tarrying a little while to make you love Him better. When He comes, you will have joy in the Lord and will rejoice with joy unspeakable. Waiting exercises our grace and tries our faith. Therefore, wait on in hope, for though the promise may tarry, it can never come too late.

Another reason why we are often most happy in our troubles is this: it is then that we have the closest relationship with God. I speak from heart knowledge and real experience. We never have such close dealings with God as when we are in the midst of tribulation. When the barn is full, man can live

WHEN YOUR GOD HIDES HIS
FACE, DO NOT SAY THAT HE HAS
FORGOTTEN YOU. HE IS BUT
TARRYING A LITTLE WHILE TO
MAKE YOU LOVE HIM BETTER.
WHEN HE COMES, YOU WILL
HAVE JOY IN THE LORD AND WILL
REJOICE WITH JOY UNSPEAKABLE.

without God. When the purse is bursting with gold, we somehow can do without so much prayer. But once your gourds are taken away, you want your God. Once the idols are cleansed out of the house, then you must go and honor Jehovah.

Some of you do not pray half as much as you ought. If you are children of God, you will have the whip. When you have that whip, you will run to your Father. It is a fine day, and the child walks before its father, but there is a lion in the road. Now he comes and takes his father's hand. He could run half a mile before him when all was fine and fair, but once a lion lurks about, it is "Father, Father!" as close as he can be. It is even so with the Christian. Let all be well, and he forgets God. Jeshurun waxed fat and began to kick against God (Deuteronomy 32:15). But when hopes are dashed, joys are blasted, infants lie in the coffin, crops are ruined, the herd is cut off from the stall, the husband's broad shoulder lies in the grave, children are fatherless—then it is that God is a God indeed.

Oh, strip me naked. Take from me all I have. Make me poor—a beggar, penniless, helpless. Dash that cistern in pieces, crush that hope, quench the stars, put out the sun, shroud the moon in darkness, and place me all alone in space without a friend or a helper. Still, "Out of the depths [will] I cry unto thee, O LORD" (Psalm 130:1). There is no cry so good as that which comes from the bottom of the mountains, no prayer half so hearty as that which comes up from the depths of the soul through deep trials and afflictions. Hence they bring us to God, and we are happier. That is the way to be happy—to live near God. So then, while troubles abound, they drive us to God, and consolations abound.

Some people call troubles "weights." Truly they are so. A ship that has large sails and a fair wind needs ballast. Troubles are the ballast of a believer. The eyes are pumps that fetch out the bilge water of his soul and keep him from sinking. But if trials are weights, I will tell you a happy secret. There is such a thing as making a weight lift you. If I have a weight chained to me, it keeps me down. Yet, give me pulleys and certain appliances, and I can make it lift me up. Yes, there is such a thing as making troubles raise me toward heaven.

A gentleman once asked his friend, concerning the friend's beautiful horse, which was feeding in the pasture with a weight attached to its leg, "Why do you tie down and restrain such a noble animal?" "Sir," replied the man's friend, "I would much sooner confine him than lose him. He is given to leaping hedges." That is why God tethers His people. He would rather restrain them than lose them. If He did not clog them, they would leap the hedges and be gone. They need a tether to prevent their straying. So God binds them with afflictions to keep them near Him, to preserve them, and have them in His presence. It is a blessed fact that as our troubles abound, so our consolations abound also.

FIVE

THE SAINTS ARE KINGS

And hast made us unto our God kings and priests;
and we shall reign on the earth.
—Revelation 5:10

Take the royal office of the saints. They are kings. They are not merely to be kings in heaven, but they are also kings on earth. For if this verse does not say so, the Bible declares it in another passage: *"Ye are a chosen generation, a royal priesthood"* (1 Peter 2:9). We are kings even now. I want you to understand that before I explain the idea.

Every saint of the living God not only has the prospect of being a king in heaven, but positively, in the sight of God, he is a king now. He must say, with regard to his brethren and himself, *"And [even now Christ] hast made us unto our God kings and priests; and we shall reign on the earth."* A Christian is a king. He is not simply like a king, but he is a king, actually and truly.

Remember the Christian's royal ancestry. What a fuss some people make about their grandfathers and grandmothers and distant ancestors! I remember seeing depicted at Trinity College the pedigree of some great lord that went back as far as Adam, and Adam was there digging the ground, the first man. It was traced all the way back. Of course I did not believe it. (I have heard of some pedigrees that go back further, but I leave that to your own common sense to believe or not.) Oh, what some would give for a pedigree in which could be found dukes, marquises, kings, and princes!

I believe, however, that it is not what our ancestors were, but what we are that will make us shine before God; that it is not so much in knowing that we have royal or priestly blood in our veins as knowing that we are an honor to our race, walking in the ways of the Lord and reflecting credit upon the church and upon the grace that makes us honorable. But since some men will glory in their descent, I will glory that the saints have the proudest ancestry in all the world. Talk of Caesars or Alexanders or tell me even of our own good Queen, and I say that I am of as proud an ancestry as her Majesty or the greatest monarch in world. I am descended from the King of Kings.

The saint may well speak of his ancestry—he may exult and glory in it—for he is the son of God, positively and actually. His mother, the church, is the bride of Jesus. He is a twice-born child of heaven, one of the blood royal of the universe. The poorest woman or man on earth, born anew in Christ, is of a royal line. Give a man the grace of God in his heart, and his ancestry is noble. I can turn back the roll of my pedigree, and I can tell

THE SAINT MAY WELL SPEAK OF
HIS ANCESTRY—HE MAY EXULT
AND GLORY IN IT—FOR HE IS THE
SON OF GOD, POSITIVELY AND
ACTUALLY. HIS MOTHER, THE
CHURCH, IS THE BRIDE OF JESUS.
HE IS A TWICE-BORN CHILD OF
HEAVEN, ONE OF THE BLOOD
ROYAL OF THE UNIVERSE. THE
POOREST WOMAN OR MAN ON
EARTH, BORN ANEW IN CHRIST,
IS OF A ROYAL LINE.

you that it is so ancient it has no beginning. It is more ancient than all the rolls of mighty men put together because, from all eternity, my Father existed. Thus, I indeed have a royal, ancient ancestry.

The saints, like monarchs, have a splendid retinue. Kings and monarchs can travel only with a great entourage of state. In olden times, they had far more magnificence than they have now, but even in these days we see much of it when royalty is abroad. There must be a select kind of horse, a splendid chariot, and outriders, with all the regalia of gorgeous pomp.

The kings of God—those whom Jesus Christ has made kings and priests unto God—also have a royal retinue. "But," you say, "I see some of them in rags and walking the earth alone, sometimes without a helper or a friend." Ah, but there is a fault in your eyes. If you had eyes to see, you would perceive a body-guard of angels always attending every one of the blood-bought family.

You remember Elijah's servant could not see anything around Elijah until his master opened his eyes. Only then he could see that there were horses and chariots around Elijah. There are horses and chariots about me. About you also, saint of the Lord, wherever you are, there are horses and chariots. In the bedchamber where I was born, angels stood to announce my birth on high. In seas of trouble, when wave after wave seems to wash over me, angels are there to lift up my head. When I come to die, when sorrowing friends carry me to the grave, angels will stand by my bier. And, when my body is put into the grave, some mighty angel will stand to guard my dust and contend for its possession with the devil. Why should I fear? I have a company of angels about me and glorious cherubim whenever I walk abroad.

Kings and princes have certain things that are theirs by positional right. For instance, her Majesty has Buckingham Palace, her other palaces, her royal crown, her scepter, and so on. But does a saint have a palace? Yes, I have a palace! Its walls are not made of marble, but of gold; its borders are garnets and precious gems; its windows are of agates; its stones are laid with fair colors; around it there is a profusion of every costly thing; rubies sparkle here and there; and pearls are but common stones within it.

Some call it a mansion, but I have a right to call it a palace also, for I am a king. It is a mansion when I look at God. It is a palace when I look at men, because it is a prince's habitation. Mark where this palace is. I am not a prince of India. I have no inheritance in any far-off land that men dream of. I have no El Dorado or Taj Mahal, but yet I have a substantial palace. Over yonder, on the hills of heaven it stands. I do not know its position among the other mansions of heaven, but there it stands. I know that if the earthly house of this tabernacle is dissolved, I have a building of God, a *"house not made with hands, eternal in the heavens"* (2 Corinthians 5:1).

Do Christians have a crown, too? Oh, yes, but they do not wear it every day. They have a crown, but their coronation day has not yet arrived. They have been anointed monarchs, they have some of the authority and dignity of monarchs, but they are not crowned monarchs yet. However, the crown is made. God will not have to order heaven's goldsmiths to fashion it later. It is made already hanging up in glory. God has *"laid up for me a crown of righteousness"* (2 Timothy 4:8). O saint, if you opened some secret door in heaven and went into the treasure chamber, you would see it filled with crowns.

When Cortez entered the palace of Montezuma, he found a secret chamber that was bricked up. So many different things were stowed away, he thought the wealth of all the world was there. If you could enter God's secret treasure house, what wealth you would see! "Are there so many monarchs, so many crowns, so many princes?" you would ask. "Yes," some bright angel would say, "And note that crown! It is yours." If you were to look within, you would read, "Made for a sinner saved by grace, whose name is ___." Then you would hardly believe your eyes, as you saw your own name engraved upon it. You are indeed a king before God, for you have a crown laid up in heaven.

Whatever other insignia belong to monarchs the saints will have. They will have robes of white; they will have harps of glory; they will have all things that become their regal state. We are indeed monarchs, you see, not mock-monarchs, clothed in purple garments of derision and scoffed at with "Hail, king of the Jews." Rather, we are real monarchs. He *"hast made us kings and priests unto our God."*

Kings are considered the most honorable among men. They are always looked up to and respected. A crowd gives way when it is announced, "A monarch is here!" I would not command much respect if I were to attempt to move about in a crowd. By contrast, if anyone should shout, "Here is the Queen!" everyone would step aside to make room for her. A monarch generally commands respect.

We think that worthy princes are the most honorable of the earth, but if you were to ask God, He would reply, "My saints in whom I delight, these are the honorable ones." Do not tell me of tinsel and baubles. Do not tell me of gold and silver. Do not tell me of diamonds and pearls. Do not tell me of ancestry and rank. Do not preach to me of pomp and power. Tell me that a man is a saint of the Lord, for then he is an honorable man. God respects him, angels respect him, and the universe one day will respect him when Christ comes to call him to his account and says, *"Well done, thou good and faithful servant…enter thou into the joy of thy Lord"* (Matthew 25:21). You may despise a child of God now, sinner. You may laugh at him and say he is a hypocrite. You may call him a ninny, an empty talker, and everything you like; but know that those titles will not mar his dignity. He is the honorable of the earth, and God esteems him as such.

But some will say, "I wish you would prove what you affirm, when you say that saints are kings. If we were kings, we would never have any sorrows. Kings are never poor as we are and never suffer as we do." Who told you so? You say if you are kings, you would live at ease. Don't kings ever suffer? Wasn't David an anointed king? Was he not hunted like a partridge on the mountains? Didn't the king himself pass over the brook Kedron and all his people weeping as he went, when his son Absalom pursued him? Was he not a monarch when he slept on the cold ground with no bed except the damp heather? Oh, yes, kings have their sorrows, and crowned heads have their afflictions. For often, "Uneasy lies the head that wears a crown." Do not expect that because you are a king, you are to have no sorrows.

"It is not for kings, O Lemuel, it is not for kings to drink wine; nor for princes strong drink" (Proverbs 31:4). And it is often so. The saints get but little wine here. It is not for kings to drink the wine of pleasure. It is not for kings to have much of the

intoxicating drink and the profusion of this world's delight. They will have joy enough up yonder, when they drink it in their Father's kingdom. Poor saint, do dwell on this. You are a king! I beseech you, do not let it slip from your mind. In the midst of your tribulation, still rejoice in it. If you have to go through the dark tunnel of infamy, for Christ's name, if you are ridiculed and reviled, still rejoice in the fact that you are a king, and all the dominions of the earth will be yours!

SIX

THE HOLY SPIRIT, ANOTHER COMFORTER

The Father...shall give you another Comforter,
that he may abide with you for ever.
John 14:16

The Holy Spirit is a very loving Comforter. Suppose I am in distress and want consolation. When some bystander hears about my sorrow, he steps in, sits down, and attempts to cheer me. He speaks soothing words, but he loves me not. He is a stranger; he knows me not at all; he has only come in to try his skill. What is the consequence? His words run over me like oil on a slab of marble. They are like the pattering rain upon the rock. They do not break my grief, which stands unmoved, because he has no love for me.

However, let someone who loves me dearly as his own life come and plead with me, then truly his words are music. They taste like honey. He knows the password to the doors of my heart, and my ear is attentive to every word. I catch the intonation of each syllable as it falls, for it is like the harmony of the harps of heaven. Oh, it is a voice in love. It speaks a language that is its own. It is an idiom and an accent that none can mimic. Wisdom cannot imitate it. Oratory cannot attain unto it. It is love alone that can reach the mourning heart. Love is the only handkerchief that can wipe the mourner's tears away.

Is not the Holy Spirit a loving Comforter? Saint, do you know how much the Holy Spirit loves you? Can you measure the love of the Spirit? Do you know how great is the affection of His soul toward you? Go, measure heaven with your span; weigh the mountains in the scales; take the ocean's water and count each drop; count the sand upon the sea's wide shore. When you have accomplished all this, you can tell how much He loves you. He has loved you long, He has loved you well, He loved you ever, and He still will love you. Surely He is the person to comfort you because He loves. Admit Him, then, to your heart, O Christian, that He may comfort you in your distress.

He is a faithful Comforter. Love sometimes proves unfaithful. Oh, sharper than a serpent's tooth is an unfaithful friend! Oh, far more bitter than the gall of bitterness is it to have a friend turn from me in my distress! Oh, woe of woes, to have one who loves me in my prosperity forsake me in the dark day of my trouble! Sad indeed, but such is not God's Spirit. He ever loves, even to the end—a faithful Comforter.

Child of God, you are in trouble. A little while ago you found Him to be a sweet and loving Comforter. You obtained

Saint, do you know how
much the Holy Spirit loves
you? He has loved you long,
He has loved you well, He
loved you ever, and He still
will love you. Surely He
is the person to comfort
you because He loves. Admit
Him, then, to your heart,
O Christian, that He may
comfort you in your distress.

relief from Him when others were but broken cisterns. He sheltered you in His bosom and carried you in His arms. Why do you distrust Him now? Away with your fears, for He is a faithful Comforter.

"But," you say, "I fear I will be sick and will be deprived of His ordinances." Nevertheless, He will visit you on your sickbed and sit by your side to give you consolation. "But I have distresses greater than you can conceive of. Wave upon wave rolls over me. Deep calls unto deep at the sound of the Eternal's waterspouts." (See Psalm 42:7.) Nevertheless, He will be faithful to His promise.

"Oh, but I have sinned." So you have, but sin cannot sever you from His love. He loves you still. Think not, downcast child of God, that because the scars of your old sins have marred your beauty that He loves you less for that blemish. No! He loved you when He foreknew you in your sin. He loved you with the knowledge of what the aggregate of your wickedness would be. He does not love you less now. Come to Him in all boldness of faith. Tell Him you have grieved Him. He will forget your roaming and will receive you again. The kisses of His love will be bestowed on you. The arms of His grace will embrace you. He is faithful, so trust Him. He will never deceive you. Trust Him, for He will never leave you.

He is an unwearied Comforter. Sometimes I have tried to comfort people who have been tried. Now and then, you may meet with the case of a nervous person. You ask, "What is your trouble?" You are told, and you try, if possible, to remove it. However, while you are preparing your artillery to batter the trouble, you find that it has shifted its quarters and is occupying a different position. You change your argument and begin again, but it is again gone. You become bewildered. You feel like Hercules cutting off the ever-growing heads of the Hydra and give up your task in despair. You meet with people whom it is impossible to comfort, bringing to mind the man who locked himself up in fetters and threw the key away so that nobody could free him.

I have found some in the fetters of despair. They cry, *"I am the man that hath seen affliction'* (Lamentations 3:1). Pity me, pity me, O my friends." The more you try to comfort such people, the worse they get. Therefore, out of all heart, we leave them to wander alone among the tombs of their former joys. But the Holy Spirit is never lacking heart with those whom He wishes to comfort. He attempts to comfort us, but we run away from the sweet cordial He offers. He gives some sweet drink to cure us, but we will not sip it. He gives some wondrous portion to charm away all our troubles, but we put it away from us. Still He pursues us. Even though we say that we will not be comforted, He says we will be. And what He has said, He does. He is not wearied by all our sins, not by all our murmuring.

How wise a Comforter is the Holy Spirit. Job had comforters, and I think he spoke the true when he said, *"Miserable comforters are ye all"* (Job 16:2). But I dare say they esteemed themselves wise. When the young man Elihu rose to speak, they thought he had a world of impudence. Were they not grave and reverend seniors? Didn't they comprehend his grief and sorrow? If they could not comfort him, who could? But they did not find out the cause.

They thought he was not really a child of God and that he was self-righteous, and then offered him the wrong remedy. It is a bad case when the doctor misdiagnoses the disease, gives a wrong prescription, and so, perhaps, kills the patient. Sometimes when we go to visit people, we mistake their disease. We want to comfort them on this point, whereas they do not require any such comfort at all, and they would be better left alone than spoiled by such unwise comforters as we are.

But how wise the Holy Spirit is! He takes the soul, lays it on the table, and dissects it in a moment. He finds out the root of the matter, He sees where the complaint is, and then He applies the knife where something is required to be taken away, or puts a plaster where the sore is. He never makes a mistake. Oh, how wise is the blessed Holy Spirit! From every comforter I turn and leave them all, for You alone give the wisest consolation.

Note how safe a Comforter the Holy Spirit is. Mark that all comfort is not necessarily safe. Over there is a very melancholy young man. You know how he became so. He stepped into the house of God and heard a powerful preacher. The Word was blessed and convicted him of sin. When he went home, his father and the rest found there was something different about him. "Oh," they said, "John is mad. He is crazy." What did his mother say? "Send him into the country for a week. Let him go to the party or to the theater." Later, they asked, "John, did you find any comfort there?" "Ah, no, they made me worse. While I was there, I thought hell might open and swallow me up." "Did you find any relief in the gaieties of the world?" "No," said he, "I thought it was idle waste of time." Alas! This is miserable comfort, but it is the comfort of the worldling.

When a Christian gets into distress, how many will recommend some pat remedy! Go hear Preacher So-and-So. Have a few friends at your house. Read a particularly consoling volume. Very likely it is the most unsafe advice in the world. The devil will sometimes come to men's souls as a false comforter and say to the soul, "What need is there to make all this ado about repentance? You are no worse than other people." He tries to make the soul believe that what is presumption is the real assurance of the Holy Spirit. Thus he deceives many by false comfort.

There have been many, like infants, destroyed by elixirs given to lull them to sleep. Many have been ruined by the cry of *"peace, peace, when there is no peace"* (Jeremiah 6:14), hearing gentle things when they ought to be stirred to the quick. Cleopatra's asp was brought in a basket of flowers, and men's ruin often lurks in fair and sweet speeches. However, the Holy Spirit's comfort is safe, and you may rest on it. Let Him speak the Word, and there is a reality about it. Let Him give the cup of consolation, and you may drink it to the bottom, for in its depth there are no dregs, nothing to intoxicate or ruin. It is all safe.

Moreover, the Holy Spirit is an active Comforter: He does not comfort by words, but by deeds. Some comfort with, *"Be ye warmed and filled; notwithstanding* [they] *give them not those things which are needful to the body"* (James 2:16). But the Holy Spirit gives. He intercedes for us. He gives us promises, He gives us grace, and so He comforts us. He is always a successful Comforter. He never attempts what He cannot accomplish.

Then He is an ever present Comforter, so that you never have to send for Him. Your God is always near you, and when you need comfort in your distress, behold, *"the word is nigh thee, even in thy mouth, and in thy heart"* (Romans 10:8). He is an ever present help in trouble.

SEVEN

PROMISES FOR THE BRUISED AND BROKEN

A bruised reed shall he not break, and smoking flax shall
he not quench, till he send forth judgment unto victory.
—Matthew 12:20

Babbling fame ever loves to talk of one man or another. There are some whose glory she trumpets forth, whose honor she extols above the heavens. Some are her favorites. Their names are carved on marble and heard in every land and every climate. Fame is not an impartial judge. She has her favored ones. Some men she extols, exalts, and almost deifies. Others, whose virtues are far greater and whose characters are more deserving of commendation, she passes by unheeded, putting the finger of silence on her lips.

You will generally find that those persons beloved by fame are men made of brass or iron and cast in a rough mold. Fame caressed Caesar because he ruled the earth with a rod of iron. Fame loved Luther because he boldly and manfully defied the Pope of Rome and with knit brow dared laugh at the thunders of the Vatican. Fame admired Knox, for he was stern and proved himself the bravest of the brave. Generally, you will find her choosing out the men of fire and mettle, who stood before their fellow creatures fearless of them; men who were made of courage, who were consolidated lumps of fearlessness, and who never knew what timidity might be.

But you know there is another class of persons equally virtuous and equally to be esteemed—perhaps even more so— those whom fame entirely forgets. You do not hear her talk of the gentle-minded Melanchthon—she says but little of him— yet he did as much, perhaps, in the Reformation as even the mighty Luther. You do not hear fame talk much of the sweet and blessed Rutherford and of the heavenly words that distilled from his lips; or of Archbishop Leighton, of whom it was said that he was never out of temper in his life.

Fame loves the rough granite peaks that defy the storm cloud. She does not care for the more humble stones in the valley on which the weary traveler rests. She wants something bold and prominent, something that courts popularity, something that stands out before the world. She does not care for those who retreat and stay in the shadows.

Hence it is, that the blessed Jesus, our adorable Master, escaped fame. No one says much about Jesus except His followers. We do not find His name written among the great and mighty men; although, in truth, He is the greatest, mightiest, holiest, purest, and best of men that ever lived. However, because He was "Gentle Jesus, meek and mild," because He was emphatically the Man whose kingdom is not of this world, because He had nothing rough about Him for He was all love, because His words were softer than butter and His utterances more gentle in their flow than oil, because no man spoke so gently as this Man, He is neglected and forgotten.

Jesus did not come to be a conqueror with His sword nor a Mohammed with his fiery eloquence. Rather, He came to speak in a *still small voice* (1 Kings 19:12) that melts the rocky heart, that binds up the broken in spirit, and that continually says, *"Come unto Me all ye that labor and are heavy laden. Take My yoke upon you, and learn of Me; for I am meek and lowly in heart: and ye shall find rest unto your souls"* (Matthew 11:28–29). Jesus Christ was all gentleness. This is why He has not been extolled among men as He otherwise would have been.

The work of God's Holy Spirit begins with bruising. In order to be saved, the fallow ground must be plowed up, the hard heart must be broken, the rock must be split apart. An old divine says there is no going to heaven without passing hard by the gates of hell—without a great deal of soul-trouble and heart-exercise. I take it then that the *"bruised reed"* is a picture of the poor sinner when first God commences his operation upon the soul. He is as a bruised reed, almost entirely broken and consumed. There is but little strength in him.

The *"smoking flax"* I take to be a backsliding Christian, one who has been a burning and shining light in his day, but by neglect of the means of grace, the withdrawal of God's Spirit, and falling into sin, his light has almost gone out. Not quite completely can it go out, for Christ says, "I will not quench it."

FAME WANTS SOMETHING BOLD AND PROMINENT, SOMETHING THAT COURTS POPULARITY, SOMETHING THAT STANDS OUT BEFORE THE WORLD. HENCE IT IS, THAT THE BLESSED JESUS, OUR ADORABLE MASTER, ESCAPED FAME. WE DO NOT FIND HIS NAME WRITTEN AMONG THE GREAT AND MIGHTY MEN; ALTHOUGH, IN TRUTH, HE IS THE GREATEST, MIGHTIEST, HOLIEST, PUREST, AND BEST OF MEN THAT EVER LIVED.

But it becomes like a lamp when ill-supplied with oil, almost useless. It is not extinguished; it still smokes. It was a useful lamp once, but now it has become as smoking flax.

Thus, I think these metaphors very likely describe the contrite sinner as a bruised reed and the backsliding Christian as smoking flax. However, I do not choose to make such a division, but will put both metaphors together and hope we may draw a few thoughts from them.

What in the world is weaker than the bruised reed or the smoking flax? Just let a wild duck light upon a reed that grows in the fen or marsh, and it snaps. Let but the foot of man brush against it, and it is bruised and broken. Every wind that comes howling across the river shakes it back and forth and nearly tears it up by the roots. I can conceive of nothing more frail or brittle, or whose existence depends more upon circumstances, than a bruised reed. Then look at a smoking flax—what is it? It has a spark within, it is true, but it is almost smothered. An infant's breath might blow it out, or the tears of a maiden quench it in a moment. Nothing has a more precarious existence than the little spark hidden in the smoking flax. Weak things are described here. Well, Christ says of them, "I will not quench the smoking flax; I will not break the bruised reed."

Some of God's children, blessed be His name, are made strong to do mighty works for Him. God has His Samsons here and there who can pull up Gaza's gates and carry them to the top of the hill. He has here and there His mighty Gideons who can go to the camp of the Midianites and overthrow their hosts. He has His mighty men who can go into the pit in winter and slay the lions.

But the majority of God's people are a timid, weak race. They are like starlings that are frightened at every movement—a little, fearful flock. If temptation comes, they fall before it. If trial comes, they are overwhelmed by it. Their frail skiffs dance up and down with every wave. When the wind comes, they are blown along like a sea bird on the crest of the billows—weak things, without strength, without force, without might, without power.

Often you may feel compelled to say, "I would, but cannot sing. I would, but cannot pray. I would, but cannot believe." You are saying that you cannot do anything; that your best resolves are weak and vain; and when you cry, "My strength renew," you feel weaker than before. You are weak, are you? Bruised reeds and smoking flax? I am glad you can come in under the denomination of weak ones, for here is a promise that He will never break or quench them, but will sustain and hold them up.

I have heard of a man who would pick up a pin as he walked along the street on the principle of economy, but I never yet heard of anyone who would stop to pick up bruised reeds. They are not worth having. Who would care to have a bruised reed, a piece of rush lying on the ground? We all despise it as worthless. And smoking flax, what is its worth? It is an offensive and noxious thing, but the worth of it is nothing. No one would give the snap of a finger either for the bruised reed or for smoking flax.

Well, then, there are many of us who are worthless things in our own estimation. There are some, who, if they could weigh themselves in the scales of the sanctuary and put their own hearts into the balance of conscience, would appear to be good-for-nothing, worthless, useless. There was a time when you thought yourselves to be the very best people in the world.

If anyone had said that you had more than you deserved, you would have balked at it and said, "I believe I am as good as other people." You thought yourselves to be something wonderful, extremely worthy of God's love and regard. But now you feel yourselves to be worthless. Sometimes you imagine God can hardly know where you are, you are such a despicable creature—so worthless, not worth His consideration. You can understand how He can look upon a minuscule organism in a drop of water or upon a grain of dust in the sunbeam or upon the insect of the summer evening. But you can hardly conceive how He can think of you because you appear so worthless—a dead blank in the world, a useless thing. You say, "What good am I? I am doing nothing. As for a minister of the Gospel, he is of some service: as for a deacon of the church, he is of some use; as for a Sunday-school teacher, he is doing some good; but of what service am I?"

You might ask the same question here. What is the use of a bruised reed? Can a man lean on it? Can a man strengthen himself by it? Can it be a pillar in a house? Can you bind it up into the pipes of Pan and make music come from a bruised reed? No! It is of no service. Of what use is smoking flax? The midnight traveler cannot be lighted by it. The student cannot read by its flame. It is of no use: men throw it into the fire to be consumed. Ah! That is how you talk of yourselves. You are good-for-nothing, and so are these things. But Christ will not throw you away because you are of no value. You do not know of what use you may be, and you cannot tell how Jesus Christ values you after all.

There is a good woman—a mother, perhaps—who says, "Well, I do not often go out. I keep house with my children and seem to be doing no good." Mother, do not say so. Your position is a high, lofty, responsible one. In training up children for the Lord, you are doing as much for His name as eloquent Apollos, who so valiantly preached the Word.

And you, poor man, all you can do is to toil from morning until night and earn just enough to enable you to live day by day. You have nothing to give away. When you go to Sunday school, you can barely read and cannot teach much. Well, unto him to whom little is given, of him little is required. (See Luke 12:48.) Do you not know that there is such a thing as glorifying God by sweeping the street crossing? If two angels were sent down to earth, one to rule an empire and the other to sweep a street, they would have no choice in the matter, as long as God ordered them. So God, in His providence, has called you to work hard for your daily bread. Do it to His glory.

EIGHT

AGAINST THE WORLD

This is the victory that overcometh the world,
even our faith.
—1 John 5:4

We know there have been great battles where nations have met in strife, and one has overcome the other. But who has read of a victory that overcame the world? Some will say that Alexander was its conqueror, but I answer that negatively. He was himself the vanquished man, even when all things were in his possession. He fought for the world and won it. Then note how it mastered its master, conquered its conqueror, and lashed the monarch who had been its scourge. See the royal youth weeping and stretching out his hands with idiotic cries for another world that he might ravage. He seemed, by outward appearances, to have overcome old earth. But in reality, within his innermost soul, the earth had conquered him, had overwhelmed him, had wrapped him in the dream of ambition, and had girdled him with the chains of covetousness, so that when he had all, he was still dissatisfied. Like a poor slave, he was dragged on at the chariot wheels of the world, crying, moaning, lamenting, because he could not win another.

Who is the man who ever overcame the world? Let him step forward. He is a Triton among the minnows. He outshines Caesar. He outmatches our own Wellington, if he can say he has overcome the world. It is so rare a thing, a victory so prodigious, a conquest so tremendous, that he who can claim to have won it may walk among his fellows, like Saul, with head and shoulders far above all. He will command our respect. His very presence will awe us into reverence. His speech will persuade us to obedience. Yielding honor to whom it is due, we will say when we hear his voice, "'Tis even as if an angel shook his wings."

Even so, the Christian overcomes the world. His is a tough battle, not one that tapestry knights might win. No easy skirmish is this that he might win, who dashed to battle on some sunny day, looked at the host, then turned his courser's rein and daintily dismounted at the door of his silken tent. This battle is not one that will be gained by the soldier who, but a raw recruit today, puts on his regimental uniform and foolishly imagines that one week of service will ensure a crown of glory. No, it is a lifelong war—a fight needing all the power of a strong heart and muscles, a contest that needs all our strength if we are to be triumphant.

If we do come off as more than conquerors, it will be said of us, as Hart said of Jesus Christ: "He had strength enough and none to spare." It is a battle at which the most courageous heart might cower, a fight about which the bravest might shake. He must remember that the Lord is on his side, and, therefore, whom should he fear; the Lord is the strength of his life, and so, of whom should he be afraid? (See Psalm 27:1.) This fight with the world is not one of brute force or physical might. If it were, we might soon win it, but it is all the more dangerous from the fact that it is a strife of mind, a contest of heart, a struggle of the spirit, a strife of the soul.

When we overcome the world in one fashion, we are not half done with our work. The world is a Proteus, changing its shape continually. Like the chameleon, it has all the colors of the rainbow. When you have bested the world in one shape, it will attack you in another. Until you die, you will always have fresh appearances of the world to wrestle with.

We rebel against the world's customs. And if we do so, what is the conduct of our enemy? The world changes her facade. "That man is a heretic; that man is a fanatic; he is a hypocrite," says the world directly. She grasps her sword, she puts a frown upon her brow, she scowls like a demon, she girds tempests around her, and she says, "The man dares defy my government; he will not do as others do. Now I will persecute him. Slander, come from the depths of hell and hiss at him! Envy, sharpen up your tooth and bite him!" She fetches up all false things, and she persecutes the man. If she can, she does it with the hand; if not, then by the tongue. She afflicts him wherever he is. She tries to ruin him in business; or, if he stands forth as the champion of the truth, then she laughs, mocks, and scorns. She lets no stone be unturned whereby she may injure him.

What is then the behavior of the Lord's warrior, when he sees the world take up arms against him, and when he sees all earth, like an army, coming to chase him and utterly destroy him? Does he yield? Does he bend? Does he cringe? Oh, no! Like Luther, he writes *cedo nulli* on his banner: "I yield to none." Then he goes to war against the world if the world goes to war against him.

The true child of God cares little for man's opinion. Says he, "Let my bread fail me. Let me be doomed to wander penniless the world over. Let me die. Each drop of blood within these veins belongs to Christ, and I am ready to shed it for His name's sake." He counts all things but loss, in order that he may win Christ and be found in Him. (See Philippians 3:8–9.) When the world's thunders roar, he smiles at the uproar while he hums his pleasant tune. When her sword comes out, he looks at it. "Ah," says he, "just as the lightning leaps from its thunderous lair, splits the clouds, and frightens the stars, but is powerless against the rock-covered mountaineer, who smiles at its grandeur, so now the world can no longer hurt me. In the time of trouble my Father hides me in His pavilion. In the secret of His tabernacle He hides me and sets me up upon a rock." Thus, again, we conquer the world, by not caring for its frowns.

"Well," says the world, "I will try another style," and this, believe me, is the most dangerous of all. A smiling world is worse than a frowning one. She says, "Since I cannot smite the man low with my repeated blows, I will take off my glove of mail, and, showing him a fair hand, I'll bid him kiss it. I will tell him I love him. I will flatter him. I will speak smooth words to him." John Bunyan well describes this Madam Bubble. She has a winning way with her. She drops a smile at the end of each of her sentences. She talks much of fair things, trying to win and woo.

THE TRUE CHILD OF GOD CARES
LITTLE FOR MAN'S OPINION. SAYS
HE, "LET MY BREAD FAIL ME. LET
ME BE DOOMED TO WANDER
PENNILESS THE WORLD OVER. LET
ME DIE. EACH DROP OF BLOOD
WITHIN THESE VEINS BELONGS
TO CHRIST, AND I AM READY TO
SHED IT FOR HIS NAME'S SAKE."
HE COUNTS ALL THINGS
BUT LOSS, IN ORDER THAT
HE MAY WIN CHRIST AND BE
FOUND IN HIM.

Oh, believe me, Christians are not so much in danger when they are persecuted as when they are admired. When we stand on the pinnacle of popularity, we may well tremble and fear. It is not when we are hissed at and hooted that we have any cause to be alarmed. It is when we are rocked in the lap of fortune and nursed upon the knees of the people. It is when all men speak well of us that woe is on us. It is not in the cold, wintry wind that I take off my coat of righteousness and throw it away. It is when the sun comes, when the weather is warm and the air balmy, that I unguardedly strip off my robes and become naked. How many a man has been made naked by the love of this world! The world has flattered and applauded him. He has drunk the flattery. It was an intoxicating draught. He has staggered, he has reeled, he has sinned, he has lost his reputation. As a comet that flashes across the sky, wanders far into space, and is lost in darkness, so does he. Great as he was, he falls. Mighty as he was, he wanders and is lost.

But the true child of God is never so. He is as safe when the world smiles as when it frowns. He cares as little for her praise as for her scorn. If he is truly praised, he says, "My deeds deserve praise, but I refer all honor to my God." Great souls know what they merit from their critics. To them it is nothing more than the giving of their daily income. Some men cannot live without a large amount of praise. If they have no more than they deserve, let them have it. If they are children of God, they will be kept steady. They will not be ruined or spoiled, but they will stand with feet like hinds' feet upon high places. "*This is the victory that overcometh the world.*"

Sometimes, the world turns jailer for a Christian. God allows affliction and sorrow until life is a prison, the world its jailer—and a wretched jailer, too. Have you ever been in trials and troubles, my friends? Has the world never come to you and said, "Poor prisoner, I have a key that will let you out. You are in financial difficulties. I will tell you how you may get free. Put that Mr. Conscience away. He just bothers you by asking whether it is a dishonest act. Never mind about him. Let him sleep. Think about the honesty after you have gotten the money and repent at your leisure." So says the world. But you say, "I cannot do the thing." "Well," says the world, "then groan and grumble. A good man like you locked up in this prison!" "No," says the Christian, "my Father sent me into want, and in His own time He will get me out. But if I die here, I will not use wrong means to escape. My Father put me here for my good, so I will not grumble. If my bones must lie here, if my coffin is to be under these stones, if my tombstone will be in the wall of my dungeon, then here will I die, rather than so much as lift a finger to get out by dishonest means." "Ah," says the world, "then you are a fool." The scorner laughs and passes on, saying, "The man has no brain, he will not do a bold thing. He has no courage. He will not launch upon the sea. He wants to go in the old beaten track of morality." So he does, for thus he overcomes the world.

I might tell of battles that have been fought. There has been many a poor maid who has worked and worked until her fingers were worn to the bone to earn a scanty living by sewing the things that we wear, not knowing that we often wear the blood and tears of poor girls. That poor maid has been tempted a thousand times to sell her purity. The evil one has tried to seduce her, but she has fought a valiant battle. Stern in her integrity, in the midst of poverty she still stands upright, "Clear as the sun, fair as the moon, and terrible as an army with banners," a heroine unconquerable by the temptations and enticements of vice.

In other cases, many a man has had the chance of being rich in an hour, affluent in a moment, if he would but clutch something that he dare not look at because God within him said, "No." The world said, "Be rich, be rich," but the Holy Spirit said, "No! Be honest. Serve your God." Oh, the stern contest and the manly combat carried on within the man's heart! But he said, "No! Could I have the stars transmuted into worlds of gold, I would not for those globes of wealth belie my principles and damage my soul." Thus he walks a conqueror. *"This is the victory that overcometh the world, even our faith."*

NINE

THE DIVINE REFUGE

The eternal God is thy refuge,
and underneath are the everlasting arms.
—Deuteronomy 33:27

The children of Israel, while they were in Egypt and the wilderness, were a visible type of God's church on earth. Moses was speaking primarily of them, but, secondarily, of all the chosen ones of God in every age. Now, as God was the shelter of His ancient people Israel, so is He the refuge of His saints through all time. First, He was eminently their shelter when they were under bondage and the yoke was heavy. When they had to make bricks without straw and the taskmasters oppressed them, the people cried unto the Lord. God heard their cry and sent to them His servant Moses.

Likewise, there often comes a time when men begin to feel the oppression of Satan. I believe that many ungodly men feel the slavery of their positions. Even some of those who are never converted have sense enough to feel at times that the service of Satan is a hard one, yielding but little pleasure and involving awful risks. Some men cannot continue making bricks without straw for long without becoming more or less conscious that they are in a house of bondage. These, who are not God's people, under the mental pressure consequent to a partial discovery of their state, turn to some form of self-righteousness or pleasure in order to forget their burden and yoke.

However, God's chosen people, moved by a higher power, are led to cry out to their God. It is one of the first signs of a chosen soul that it seems to know as if by heavenly instinct where its true refuge is. You may recollect that, although you knew but little of Christ, in doctrinal matters you were very dark, and you did not understand even your own need, yet there was something in you that allowed you to see that only at the mercy seat could you find refuge.

Before you were a Christian, your bedside was the witness to many flowing tears, when your aching heart poured itself out before God, perhaps in strains like these: "O God, I want something. I do not know what it is I want, but I feel a heaviness of spirit. My mind is burdened, and I feel that You alone can unburden me. I know that I am a sinner. Oh, that You would forgive me! I hardly understand the plan of salvation, but one thing I know, that I want to be saved. I arise and go to my Father. My heart pants to make You my refuge." I say that this is one of the first indications that such a soul is one of God's chosen. It is true, just as it was of Israel in Egypt, that God is the refuge of His people, even when they are under the yoke.

When captivity is led captive (Psalm 68:18), the eternal God becomes the refuge of His people from their sins. The Israelites were brought out of Egypt. They were free. Admittedly, they did not know where they were marching, yet their chains were snapped. They were emancipated and no longer needed to call anyone "Master." Yet, Pharaoh was angry and pursued them. With his horses and chariots, he hastened after them. The enemy said, *"I will pursue, I will overtake, I will divide the spoil; my lust shall be satisfied upon them"* (Exodus 15:9).

Similarly, there is a period in the spiritual life when sin labors to drag back the sinner who has newly escaped from it. Like hosts ready for battle, all the poor sinner's past iniquities hurry after him and overtake him in a place where his way is hedged in. The poor fugitive would escape, but he cannot. What, then, must he do? Remember that at that point Moses cried unto the Lord. When nothing else could be found to afford shelter to the poor escaped slaves, when the Red Sea rolled before them and mountains shut them in on either side, and an angry foe pursued them, there was one road that was not stopped up. That was the king's highway upward to the throne, the way to their God. Therefore, they began at once to travel that road, lifting up their hearts in humble prayer to God, trusting that He would deliver them. You know the story: how the uplifted rod divided the watery deeps, how the people passed through the sea as a horse through the wilderness, and how the Lord brought all the hosts of Egypt into the depths of the sea that He might utterly destroy them, so that not one of them was left, and those who had seen them one day saw them no more.

In this sense, God is still the refuge of His people. Our sins, which pursued us so hotly, have been drowned in the depths of the Savior's blood. They sank to the bottom like stones, the depths have covered them, and not one of them is left. We, standing upon the shore in safety, can shout in triumph over our drowned sins, *"Sing unto the Lord for He hath triumphed gloriously; [all our iniquities] hath He thrown into the sea"* (Exodus 15:1).

While God is thus the refuge of His people under the yoke, and when sin seeks to overcome them, He is also their refuge in times of want. The children of Israel journeyed into the wilderness, but there was nothing for them to eat there. The arid sand yielded neither leeks nor garlic nor cucumbers. No brooks or rivers like the Nile were there to quench their thirst. They would have famished if they had been left to depend on the natural productions of the soil. They came to Marah, where the well water was very bitter. At other stations there were no wells at all, even with bitter water. What then? The unfailing refuge of God's people in the wilderness was prayer. Moses, their representative, always took himself to the Most High, at times falling upon his face in agony, and at other seasons climbing to the top of the hill, to plead in solemn communion with God that He would deliver the people.

You have heard often how men ate angels' food in the desert, how Jehovah rained bread from heaven upon His people in the howling wilderness, and how He smote the rock and waters gushed forth. You have not forgotten how the strong wind blew and brought them flesh so that they ate and were satisfied. Israel had no need unsupplied. Their garments did not wear out. Though they went through the wilderness, their feet were

GOD IS STILL THE REFUGE OF
HIS PEOPLE. OUR SINS, WHICH
PURSUED US SO HOTLY, HAVE
BEEN DROWNED IN THE DEPTHS
OF THE SAVIOR'S BLOOD. THEY
SANK TO THE BOTTOM LIKE
STONES, THE DEPTHS HAVE
COVERED THEM, AND NOT ONE
OF THEM IS LEFT. WE, STANDING
UPON THE SHORE IN SAFETY, CAN
SHOUT IN TRIUMPH OVER OUR
DROWNED SINS.

not sore. God supplied all their wants. We in our land must go to the baker, the butcher, the clothier, and many others in order to equip ourselves, but the men of Israel went to God for everything. We have to store up our money and buy this in one place and that in the other, but the eternal God was their refuge and their resort for everything. In every time of want, they had nothing to do but to lift up their voices to Him.

Now it is just so with us spiritually. Faith sees our position today to be the same as the children of Israel then: whatever our wants are, "*the eternal God is* [our] *refuge.*" God has promised you that your bread and water will be given to you. He who supplies spiritual wants will not deny temporal ones. The mighty Master will never suffer you to perish while He has it in His power to succor you. Go to Him, whatever may be the trouble that weighs you down. Do not suppose your case too bad, for nothing is too hard for the Lord.

Do not think that He will refuse to undertake temporal needs as well as the spiritual wants. He cares for you in all things. In everything you are to give thanks, and surely in everything by prayer and supplication, you may make known your wants unto God. (See Philippians 4:6). In times when the cruse of oil is ready to fail and the handful of meal is all but spent, then go to the all-sufficient God. You will find that those who trust in Him will not lack any good thing. (See Psalm 34:10).

Furthermore, our God is the refuge of His saints when their enemies rage. When the host was passing through the wilderness, they were suddenly attacked by the Amalekites. Unprovoked, these marauders of the desert set upon them and smote many, but what did Israel do? The people did not ask to have a strong body of horsemen hired out of the land of Egypt for their refuge. Even if they did wish it, he who was their wise leader, Moses, looked to another arm than that of man, for he cried unto God. How glorious is that picture of Moses, with uplifted hands, upon the top of the hill giving victory to Joshua in the plain below. Those uplifted arms were worth ten thousand men to the hosts of Israel; no, twice ten thousand had not so easily won a victory as did those two extended arms, which brought down Omnipotence Himself from heaven. This was Israel's master weapon of war, her confidence in God. Joshua went forth with mighty men of war, but the Lord, Jehovah-Nissi, is the banner of the fight and the giver of the victory.

Thus, *the eternal God is* [our] *refuge.* When our foes rage, we need not fear their fury. Let us not seek to be without enemies, but let us take our case and spread it before God. We cannot be in such a position that the weapons of our foes can hurt us, while the promise stands true: *"No weapon that is formed against thee shall prosper, and every tongue that riseth against thee in judgment thou shalt condemn"* (Isaiah 54:17). Though earth and hell should unite in malice, the eternal God is our fortress and stronghold, securing to us an everlasting refuge.

TEN

THE USE OF CHASTISEMENT

My son, despise not thou the
chastening of the Lord.
—Hebrews 12:5

God's people can never by any possibility be punished for their sins. God has punished them already in the person of Christ. Christ, their substitute, has endured the full penalty for all their guilt, and neither the justice nor the love of God can ever exact again what Christ has paid. Punishment can never happen to a child of God in the judicial sense. He can never be brought before God as his Judge, charged with guilt, because that guilt was long ago transferred to the shoulders of Christ and the punishment was exacted at the hands of his Surety.

But yet, while the sin cannot be punished, while the Christian cannot be condemned, he can be chastised. While he will never be arraigned before God's bar as a criminal and punished for his guilt, yet he now stands in a new relationship—that of a child to his parent. As a son, he may be chastised because of sin. Foolishness is bound up in the heart of all God's children, and the Father's rod must bring that folly out of them (Proverbs 22:15).

It is essential to observe the distinction between punishment and chastisement. Both may agree as to the nature of the suffering: the suffering under one may be as great as under the other. The sinner, while he is punished for his guilt, may suffer no more in this life than the Christian who is only chastised by his parent. They do not differ as to the nature of the affliction, but they differ in the mind of the one who afflicts and in the relationship of the person who is afflicted. God punishes the sinner on his own account because He is angry with the sinner. His justice must be avenged, His law must be honored, and His commands must have their dignity maintained.

However, God does not punish the believer on his own account. It is on the Christian's account to do him good. He afflicts him for his profit. God lays on the rod for His child's advantage. He has a good intention toward the person who receives the chastisement. In punishment, the design is simply with God for God's glory; in chastisement, it is with the person chastised for his good and his spiritual profit and benefit. Besides, punishment is laid on a man in anger. God strikes him in wrath, but when He afflicts His child, chastisement is applied in love, all of His strokes are put there by the hand of love. The rod has been baptized in deep affection before it is laid on the believer's back. God does not afflict willingly or grieve us for nothing. Rather, His chastising is out of love and affection, because He perceives that if He leaves us unchastised, we will bring upon ourselves misery ten-thousandfold greater than we will suffer by His slight rebukes and the gentle blows of His hand.

Understand this from the very start: whatever your trouble or your affliction, there cannot be anything punitive in it. You must never say, "God is punishing me for my sin." You have fallen from your steadfastness when you talk so. God cannot do that. He has done it once for all: *"The chastisement of our peace was upon Him, and with His stripes we are healed"* (Isaiah 53:5).

God is chastising you, not punishing you. He is correcting you in measure, not smiting you in wrath. There is no hot displeasure in His heart. Even though His brow may be wrinkled, there is no anger in His heart. Even though His eye may have closed upon you, He does not hate you. He loves you still. He is not wrathful with His heritage, for He sees no sin in Jacob, neither iniquity in Israel, who are considered in the person of Christ. It is simply because He loves you, because you are sons, that He therefore chastises you.

Why should you murmur against the dispensations of your heavenly Father? Can He treat you harder than you deserve? Consider what a rebel you were, but He has pardoned you. Surely, if He chooses now to lay the rod upon you, you need not cry out. Among the Roman emperors of old, it was the custom when they set a slave at liberty to give him a blow on the head and then say, "Go free!" This blow that your Father gives you is a token of your liberty.

Do you grumble because He smites you rather hardly? After all, are not His strokes fewer than your crimes and lighter

GOD IS CHASTISING YOU,
NOT PUNISHING YOU. HE IS
CORRECTING YOU IN MEASURE,
NOT SMITING YOU IN WRATH.
THERE IS NO HOT DISPLEASURE
IN HIS HEART. EVEN THOUGH HIS
BROW MAY BE WRINKLED, THERE
IS NO ANGER IN HIS HEART. EVEN
THOUGH HIS EYE MAY HAVE
CLOSED UPON YOU, HE DOES NOT
HATE YOU. HE LOVES YOU STILL.

than your guilt? Are you smitten as hard as your sins deserve? Consider all the corruption that is in your heart, and then will you wonder that so much of the rod is needed to drive it out? Weigh yourself, and discern how much dross is mingled with your gold. Do you think the fire is too hot to bring up the dross you have? Why, I think the furnace is not hot enough. There is too much dross, too little fire. The rod is not laid on hard enough, for that proud spirit of yours proves that your heart is not thoroughly sanctified. Though your heart may be right with God, your words do not sound like it, and your actions do not portray the holiness of your nature. It is the old Adam within you that is groaning.

Take heed if you murmur, for it will go hard with murmurers. God always chastises His children twice if they do not bear the first blow patiently. I have often heard a father say, "Boy, if you cry for that, you will really have something to cry for by and by." So, if we murmur at a little, God gives us something that will make us cry. If we groan for nothing, He will give us something that will make us groan. Sit down in patience. *"Despise not the chastening of the Lord."* Do not be angry with Him, for He is not angry with you. Do not say that He deals so hardly with you. Let humility rise up and speak, "It is well, O Lord! You are just in Your chastising, for I have sinned. Righteous are You in your blows, for I need them to bring me near to You. If You leave me uncorrected and unchastised, I, a poor wanderer, must pass away to the gulf of death and sink into the pit of eternal perdition." The first sense in which we may despise the chastening of the Lord is that we may murmur under it.

There are certain things that happen to us in life that we immediately set down as a providence. If a grandfather of ours should die and leave us five hundred pounds, what a merciful providence that would be! If by some extraordinary event in business we were suddenly to accumulate a fortune, that would be a blessed providence! If an accident happens, but we are preserved and our limbs are not hurt, that is always a providence.

But suppose we were to lose five hundred pounds, would not that be a providence? Suppose our establishment should break up and business fail, would not that be a providence? Suppose we should break a leg in the accident, would not that be a providence? Here is the difficulty: it is always a providence when it is a good thing, but why is it not a providence when it does not happen to be just as we please? Surely it is so. If the one thing is ordered by God, so is the other. It is written, "*I form the light and create darkness: I make peace and create evil: I, the* Lord, *do all these things*" (Isaiah 45:7). But I question whether it is not despising the chastening of the Lord when we set a prosperous providence before an adverse one, for I do think that an adverse providence ought to be the cause of as much thankfulness as a prosperous one. If it is not, we are violating the command, "*In everything give thanks*" (1 Thessalonians 5:18).

However, we say, "Of what use will such a trial be to me? I cannot see that it can by any possibility be useful to my soul. Here I was growing in grace just now, but there is something that has dampened all my ardor and overthrown my zeal. Just now I was on the mount of assurance, and God has brought me to the valley of humiliation. Can that be any good to me? A few weeks ago I had wealth, and I distributed it in the cause of God. Now I have none. What can be the use of that? All these things are against me." Now, you are despising the chastening of the Lord, when you say that it is of no use.

No child thinks the rod is of much value. Anything in the house is of more use than that rod in his opinion. If you were to ask the child what part of the household furniture could be dispensed with, he would like chairs, tables, and everything else to remain except the rod, which he does not think of any good whatever. He despises the rod, and so do we. We think it cannot benefit us. We want to get rid of the rod and turn it away. *"My son, despise not thou the chastening of the Lord."*

Let me show you how wrong you are. Does your ignorance intend to say that God is unwise? I thought it was written that He was too wise to err. I did think that you knew that He was too good to be unkind. Does your tiny wisdom assign to itself the chair of honor? Does your finite knowledge stand up before your Maker and tell Him He is unwise in what He does? Will you dare to say that one of His purposes will be unfulfilled, that He does an unwise act? You are impudently arrogant if you speak in such a manner! Do not say so, but bend meekly down before His superior wisdom and say, "O God, I believe that in the darkness You are brewing light, that in the storm clouds You are gathering sunshine, that in the mines You are fashioning diamonds, and in the beds of the sea You are making pearls. I believe that however unfathomable may be Your plans, yet they have a bottom. Though it is in the whirlwind and in the storm, You have a way that is good and righteous altogether. I would not have You alter one atom of your dispensations. It shall be just as You will. I bow before You and give my ignorance the command to hold its tongue and to be silenced while Your wisdom speaks words of right."

"My son, despise not thou the chastening of the Lord" by thinking that it can be of no possible service to you. Many men have

been corrected by God, and that correction has been in vain. I have known Christian men—men who have committed some sin. God, by the rod, would have shown them the evil of that sin. They have been smitten and seen the sin, but never afterward did they correct it. That is despising the chastening of the Lord. When a father chastises a son for anything he has done, and the boy does it again directly, it shows that he despises his father's chastening. So also have we seen believers who have had an error in their lives, and God has chastened them on account of it, but they have continued to repeat the error.

You will remember the case of Eli. God chastened him once when He sent Samuel to tell him dreadful news, that because he had not reproved his children, those children would be destroyed. But Eli kept on the same as ever. He despised the chastening of the Lord although his ears were made to tingle. In a little while God did something else for him. His sons were taken away, and then it was too late to mend for the children were gone. The time in which he might have reformed his character had passed away.

How many of you get chastened by God, but do not hear the rod? There are many deaf souls that do not hear God's rod. Many Christians are blind and cannot see God's purposes. When God would take some folly out of them, the folly is still retained.

Not every affliction benefits the Christian, only a sanctified affliction. Not every trial purifies an heir of light, only a trial that God Himself sanctifies by His grace. Take heed if God is trying you, that you search and find out the reason. Are the consolations of God small with you? Then, there is some reason for it. Have you lost that joy you once felt? There is some cause for it.

Many a man would not have suffered half as much if he had looked for the cause of it. I have sometimes walked a mile or two almost limping because there was a stone in my shoe, but I did not stop to check it. Many a Christian goes limping for years because of the stones in his shoe, but if he would only stop to look for them, he would be relieved. What is the sin that is causing you pain? Get it out in the open and repent of it, for if you do not, you have not regarded this admonition that speaks to you as unto sons: *"My son, despise not thou the chastening of the Lord."*

ELEVEN

RESPONSIBILITY AND SUCCESS

We are unto God a sweet savor of Christ,
in them that are saved, and in them that perish.
—2 Corinthians 2:15

The minister is not responsible for his success. He is responsible for what he preaches, he is accountable for his life and actions, but he is not responsible for other people. If I but preached God's Word, if there never were a soul saved, the King would say, "*Well done, good and faithful servant!*" (Matthew 25:23). If I only tell my message, even if none listen to it, He would say, "You have fought the good fight. Receive your crown." Truly hear the words of the text, "*We are unto God a sweet savor of Christ, in them that are saved, and in them that perish.*"

This will be apparent if I simply tell you what a gospel minister is called in the Bible. On occasion he is called an ambassador. Now, for what is an ambassador responsible? He goes to a country as a fully authorized diplomat. He carries terms of peace to the conference table. He uses all his talents for his ruler. He tries to show that war is inimical to the prosperity of the differing countries. He endeavors to bring about peace, but the other rulers haughtily refuse it. When he comes home, his governor asks, "Why did you not make peace?" "Why, my lord," he replies, "I told them the terms, but they said nothing." "Well, then," his commander would say, "you have done your duty. I cannot condemn you if the war continues."

Again, the minister of the Gospel is called a fisherman. Now a fisherman is not responsible for the quantity of fish he catches, but for the way he fishes. That is a mercy for some ministers, I am sure, for they have not caught fish or even attracted any around their nets. They have been spending their lives fishing with the most elegant silk lines and gold and silver hooks. They always use nicely polished phrases, but the fish do not bite for all that, whereas we of a rougher presentation have put the hook into the jaws of hundreds. However, if we cast the gospel net in the right place, even if we catch none, the Master will find no fault with us. He will say, "Fisherman! Did you labor? Did you throw the net into the sea in the time of storms?" "Yes, my Lord, I did." "What have you caught?" "Only one or two." "Well, I could have sent you a shoal, if it so pleased Me. It is not your fault. I give in My sovereignty where I please, or withhold when I choose. But as for you, you have labored well. Therefore, here is your reward."

Sometimes the minister is called a sower. No farmer expects a sower to be responsible for the harvest. All he is responsible for is this: does he sow the seed, and does he sow the right seed?

If he scatters it on good soil, then he is happy. But if it falls by the wayside and the fowls of the air devour it, who will blame the sower? Could he help it? No, he did his duty. He scattered the seed broadcast, and there he left it. Who is to blame? Surely not the sower.

So if a minister comes to heaven with but one sheaf on his shoulder, his Master will say, "O reaper! Once a sower! Where did you gather your sheaf?" "My Lord, I sowed upon the rock, and it would not grow. Only one seed on a chance Sabbath morning was blown a little awry by the wind, and it fell upon a prepared heart, and this is my one sheaf." "Hallelujah!" the angelic choirs resound, "One sheaf from a rock is more honor to God than a thousand sheaves from a good soil. Therefore, let him take his seat as near the throne as that man, who, stooping beneath his many sheaves, comes from some fertile land, bringing his sheaves with him."

I believe that if there are degrees in glory, they will not be in proportion to success, but in proportion to the earnestness of our endeavors. If we, as ministers, mean right and strive to do right with all our hearts (even if we never see any effect), still will we receive the crown.

But how much happier is the man who will have it said about him in heaven, "He shines forever, because he was wise and won many souls unto righteousness." It is always my greatest joy to believe that, when I enter heaven in future days, I will see heaven's gates open. In will come a smiling person who, looking me in the face, will pass along to God's throne and bow down before Him. When he has paid his homage and his adoration to the Almighty, he may come to me and clasp my hand, though unknown to me. If there were tears in heaven, surely I would weep, and he would say, "Brother, from your lips I heard the word. Your voice first admonished me of my sin. Here I am. You were the instrument of my salvation."

As gates open one after another, still will they come in—souls ransomed, souls redeemed—and for each one of these a star, for each one of these another gem in the diadem of glory, for each one of them another honor and another note in the song of praise. *"Blessed are the dead which die in the Lord...saith the Spirit, that they may rest from their labors; and their works do follow them"* (Revelation 14:13).

What will happen to some Christians if crowns in heaven are measured in value by the souls that are saved? Some will have a crown in heaven without a single star in it. I read a little while ago a piece about a starless crown in heaven—a man in heaven with a crown without a star! Not one saved by him! He will sit in heaven as happy as can be because sovereign mercy saved him, but to be in heaven without a single star! Mother, what would you say to be in heaven without one of your children to deck your brow with a star? Minister, what would you say to be a polished preacher and yet have no star? Writer, will it become you to have written as gloriously as Milton if you are found in heaven without a star?

I am afraid we pay too little attention to this. Men will sit down and write huge tomes, so that they may have them put in libraries forever and have their names handed down by fame, but how many are looking to win stars forever in heaven? Toil on, child of God, toil on. If you wish to serve God, your bread that you cast upon the waters will be found after many days. If you *"send forth the feet of the ox and the ass"* (Isaiah 32:20), you

I BELIEVE THAT IF THERE ARE
DEGREES IN GLORY, THEY WILL
NOT BE IN PROPORTION TO
SUCCESS, BUT IN PROPORTION
TO THE EARNESTNESS OF OUR
ENDEAVORS. IF WE, AS MINISTERS,
MEAN RIGHT AND STRIVE TO DO
RIGHT WITH ALL OUR HEARTS
(EVEN IF WE NEVER SEE
ANY EFFECT), STILL WILL WE
RECEIVE THE CROWN.

will reap a glorious harvest in that day when He comes to gather in His elect. The minister is not responsible for his success.

Still, to preach the Gospel is high and solemn work. The minister has been very often degraded into a trade. In these days men are taken and made into ministers who would have made good captains at sea, who could have waited well at the counter, but who were never intended for the pulpit. They are selected by man. They are crammed full with literature. They are educated up to a certain point. They are turned out already dressed. People call them ministers. I wish them all God's blessing, every one of them. As good Joseph Irons used to say, "God be with many of them, if it be only to make them hold their tongues."

Man-made ministers are of no use in this world, and the sooner we get rid of them the better. Their way is this: they prepare their sermon manuscripts very carefully, then read them on Sunday most sweetly in *sotto voce*, and so the people go away pleased. However, that is not God's way of preaching. If it were so, then I am capable of preaching forever. I can buy manuscript sermons for a shilling, provided they have been preached fifty times before. However, if I use them for the first time, the price is a guinea or more. But that is not God's way.

Preaching God's Word is not what some seem to think—mere child's play—a mere business or trade to be taken up by anyone. A man ought to feel first that he has a solemn call to it. Next, he ought to know that he really possesses the Spirit of God and that when he speaks there is an influence upon him that enables him to speak as God would have him. Otherwise, out of the pulpit he should go directly. He has no right to be there, even if the living is his own property. He has not been called to preach God's truth, and unto him God says, "*What hast thou to do to declare My statutes?*" (Psalm 50:16).

What is there difficult about preaching God's Gospel? Well, it must be somewhat hard, because Paul asked, "*Who is sufficient for these things?*" (2 Corinthians 2:16). First I will tell you that it is difficult because it is so hard not to be warped by your own prejudices in preaching the Word. You want to say a stern thing, but your heart says, "Master, in so doing you will condemn yourself also!" Then the temptation is not to say it. Another persuasion is that you are afraid of displeasing the rich in your congregations. You think, "If I say this thing, So-and-So will be offended. Such a person does not approve of that doctrine. I had better leave it out." Or, perhaps you will happen to win the applause of the multitude and must not say anything that will displease them, for if they cry "Hosanna" today, they will cry "Crucify, crucify," tomorrow. All these things work on a minister's heart. He is a man, and he feels it.

Then comes again the sharp knife of criticism, along with the arrows of those who hate the minister and hate his Lord. He cannot help feeling it sometimes. He may put on his armor and cry, "I care not about your malice," but there were seasons when the archers sorely grieved even Joseph. Then the minister stands in another danger, lest he should come out and defend himself, because he is a great fool whoever tries to do it. He who lets his detractors alone, and like the eagle cares not for the chattering of the sparrows, or like the lion will not turn aside to rend the snarling jackal—he is the man, and he will be honored. The danger is that we want to set ourselves right.

Who is capable of steering clear of these rocks of danger? *"Who is sufficient for these things?"* Who is able to stand up and to proclaim, Sunday after Sunday, weekday after weekday, *"the unsearchable riches of Christ"* (Ephesians 3:8)?

TWELVE

DEVOTIONS IN THE NIGHT

With my soul have I desired thee in the night.
—Isaiah 26:9

Night appears to be a time particularly favorable to devotion. Its solemn stillness helps to free the mind from the perpetual din that the cares of the world will bring around it. Looking down from heaven on us, the stars shine as if they would attract us up to God. I do not know how you may be affected by the solemnities of midnight; however, when I have sat alone musing on the great God and the mighty universe, I have felt indeed that I could worship Him, for night seemed to be spread abroad as a temple for adoration, while the moon walked as high priest amid the stars and the worshippers. I myself joined in the silent song that they sang unto God:

> *O Lord, how great are thy works!...When I consider thy*
> *heavens, the work of thy fingers, the moon and the stars*
> *which thou hast ordained; what is man that thou are mind-*
> *ful of him? and the son of man, that thou visitest him?*
>
> (Psalm 92:5; 8:3–4)

I find that this sense of the power of midnight not only acts upon religious men, but upon others as well. There is a certain poet, whose character I could scarcely reprove too much, a man very far from understanding true religion. I suppose I might justly classify him an infidel or a libertine of the worst order. Yet he says concerning night in one of his poems:

> 'Tis midnight on the mountains brown,
>   The cold round moon shines deeply down;
>   Blue roll the waters, blue the sky
>   Spreads like an ocean hung on high,
>   Bespangled with those isles of light,
>   So wildly, spiritually bright;
>   Who ever gazed upon them shining,
>   And turning to earth without repining,
>   Nor wish'd for wings to flee away,
>   And mix with their eternal ray.

Even with the most irreligious person, a man farthest from spiritual thought, it seems that there is some power in the grandeur and stillness of night to draw him up to God. I trust many of us can say, like David and Isaiah, "I have been with You continually, I have meditated upon Your name in the night watches, and with my soul have I desired You in the night." (See Psalm 73:23; 63:6; and Isaiah 26:9.)

The Christian man does not always have a bright shining sun. He has seasons of darkness and night. True, God's Word says: *"Her ways are ways of pleasantness, and all her paths are peace"* (Proverbs 3:17). It is a great truth that religion—the true religion of the living God—is calculated to give a man joy below, as well as bliss above. But notwithstanding, experience tells us that if the course of the just is *"as the shining light, that shineth more and more unto the perfect day"* (Proverbs 4:18), yet sometimes that light may be eclipsed. At certain times, darkness and clouds cover the sun, and the man of God beholds no clear, shining daylight, but walks in darkness and sees no light.

Now, there are many who have rejoiced in the presence of God for a season. They have basked in the sunshine God has been pleased to give them in the earlier stages of their Christian career. They have walked along the *"green pastures,"* by the side of *"still waters,"* and suddenly—within a month or two—they find that glorious sky is clouded. Instead of *"green pastures,"* they have to tread the sandy desert. In the place of *"still waters,"* they find streams brackish to their taste and bitter to their spirits. They say, "Surely, if I were a child of God, this would not happen." Oh, say not so, you who are walking in darkness!

The best of God's saints have their nights. The dearest of His children have to walk through a weary wilderness. There is not a Christian who has enjoyed perpetual happiness. There is no believer who can always sing a song of joy. Not every lark can always carol, not every star can always be seen, and not every Christian is always happy.

Perhaps the King of saints gave you a season of great joy at first because you were a raw recruit, and He would not put you into the roughest part of the battle when you had first enlisted.

THE BEST OF GOD'S SAINTS HAVE
THEIR NIGHTS. THE DEAREST OF
HIS CHILDREN HAVE TO WALK
THROUGH A WEARY WILDERNESS.
NOT EVERY LARK CAN ALWAYS
CAROL, NOT EVERY STAR CAN
ALWAYS BE SEEN, AND NOT EVERY
CHRISTIAN IS ALWAYS HAPPY.

You were a tender plant, and He nursed you in the hothouse until you could stand severe weather. You were a young child, and therefore He wrapped you in furs and clothed you in the softest mantle. But now you have become strong, and the case is different. Capuan holidays do not suit Roman soldiers, and they would not agree with Christians. We need clouds and darkness to exercise our faith, to cut off self-dependence, and to make us put more faith in Christ and less in evidence, less in experience, less in mental states and feelings. The best of God's children—I repeat it again for the comfort of those who are suffering with depression—have their nights.

Sometimes it is a night over the whole church at once. There are times when Zion is under a cloud, when the fine gold becomes dim and the glory of Zion is departed. There are seasons when we do not hear the clear preaching of the Word, when doctrines are withheld, when the glory of the Lord God of Jacob is dim, when His name is not exalted, when the traditions of men are taught instead of the inspirations of the Holy Spirit. Such a season is it when the whole church is dark. Of course, each Christian participates in it. He goes about weeping and crying, "O God, how long will Zion be oppressed? How long will her shepherds be as *dumb dogs, they cannot bark*' (Isaiah 56:10)? Will her watchmen always be blind? Will the silver trumpet sound no more? Will not the voice of the Gospel be heard in her streets?"

Oh, there are seasons of darkness to the entire church! God grant that we may not have to pass through another, but that, starting from this time, the sun may rise never to set, until, like a sea of glory, the light of brilliance will spread from pole to pole!

At other times, this darkness over the soul of the Christian rises from temporal distresses. He may have had a misfortune, as it is called: something has gone wrong in his business, or an enemy has done somewhat against him; death has struck down a favored child, or bereavement has snatched away the darling of his bosom; the crops are blighted; the winds refuse to bear his ships homeward; a vessel strikes upon a rock, and another founders. All goes ill with him. Like a gentleman who called to see me, he may be able to say, "Sir, I prospered far more when I was a worldly man than I have done since I have become a Christian, for everything has appeared to go wrong with me since then. I thought," he said, "that religion had the promise of this life as well as of that which is to come." I told him that it had, and so it would be in the end.

However, we must remember there was one great legacy that Christ left His people, and I was glad he had come in for a share of it: "*In me ye might have peace* [but] *in the world ye shall have tribulation*" (John 16:33). Yes! You may be troubled about this. You may be saying, "Look at So-and-So. See how he spreads himself like a chestnut tree. He is an extortioner and wicked man, yet everything he does prospers." You may even observe his death and say, "There are no bands in his death." "*They are not in trouble as other men, neither are they plagued like other men*" (Psalm 73:5). God has set them in slippery places, but He casts them down to destruction.

Better to have a Christian's days of sorrow than a worldling's days of mirth. Better to have a Christian's sorrows than a worldling's joys. Happier it is to be chained in a dungeon with a Paul than reign in the palace with an Ahab. Better to be a child of God in poverty than a child of Satan in riches. Cheer up, then, you downcast spirit, if this is your trial. Remember that many saints have passed through the same, and the best, most eminent believers have had their nights.

Christian men very frequently have their nights, but a Christian man's religion will keep its color in the night. *"With my soul have I desired thee in the night."* What a lot of silver-slippered religion we have in this world! Men will follow Christ when everyone cries, "Hosanna! Hosanna!" The multitude will crowd around the Man then, and they will take Him by force and make Him a king when the sun shines and a soft wind blows. They are like the plants upon the rock, which sprang up and for a little while were green, but when the sun had risen with fervent heat straightway withered away.

Demas and Mr. Hold-the-World, and a great many others, are very pious people in easy times. They will always go with Christ by daylight and will keep in company so long as fashion gives religion the doubtful benefit of its patronage. But they will not go with Him in the night. There are some goods whose color you can only see in sunlight— and there are many professing believers whose colors you can only see by the light of day. If they were in the night of trouble and persecutions, you would find that there was very little in them. They are good by daylight, but they are bad by night.

Do you not know that the best test of a Christian is the night? The nightingale, if she would sing by day when every goose is cackling, would be considered no better a musician than the wren. If a Christian remained steadfast only by daylight when every coward is bold, what would he be? There would be no beauty in his courage, no glory in his bravery. But it is because he can sing in the night, sing in times of trouble, sing

BETTER TO HAVE A CHRISTIAN'S
DAYS OF SORROW THAN A
WORLDLING'S DAYS OF MIRTH.
BETTER TO HAVE A CHRISTIAN'S
SORROWS THAN A WORLDLING'S
JOYS. HAPPIER IT IS TO BE
CHAINED IN A DUNGEON WITH A
PAUL THAN REIGN IN THE PALACE
WITH AN AHAB. BETTER TO BE A
CHILD OF GOD IN POVERTY THAN
A CHILD OF SATAN IN RICHES.

when he is driven to despair, which proves his sincerity. The testing has its glory in the night. The stars are not visible by daylight, but they become apparent when the sun sets.

There are many Christians whose piety did not evidence itself much when they were in prosperity, but will be shown in adversity. I have marked it in some of my brethren when they were in deep trial. I had not heard them speak much about Christ before, but when God's hand had robbed them of their comfort, I remember that I could discern their true beliefs infinitely better than I could before.

Nothing can bring our religion out better than trials. Grind the diamond a little, and you will see it glisten. Do but put trouble on the Christian, and his endurance of it will prove him to be of the true seed of Israel.

All that the Christian wants in the night is his God. *"With my soul have I desired thee in the night."* By day there are many things that a Christian will desire besides his Lord, but in the night he wants nothing but his God.

I cannot understand how this happens, unless it is to be accounted for by the corruption of our spirits. When everything is going well with us, we are setting our affection first on this object and then on another; and that burning desire, which is as insatiable as death and as deep as hell, never rests satisfied. We are always wanting something, always desiring a yet-beyond. But if you place a Christian in trouble, you will find that then he does not want gold or carnal honor—then he only wants his God.

I suppose he is like the sailor. When he sails along smoothly, he loves to have fair weather and wants this and that with which to amuse himself on deck. But when the winds blow, all that he wants is the haven. He does not desire anything else. The biscuit may be moldy, but he does not care. The water may be brackish, but he does not care. He does not think of it in the storm. He only thinks about the haven then.

So it goes with the Christian: when he is going along smoothly he wants this and that comfort; he is aspiring after this position or is wanting to obtain that promotion. But let him once doubt his interest in Christ—let him once get into some distress so that it is very dark—and all he will feel then is, *"With my soul have I desired thee in the night."*

When a little girl is put to bed, she may lie quietly while there is light, looking at the trees that shake against the window and admiring the stars that are coming out. But when it gets dark and the child is still awake, she cries for her parent. She cannot be amused by anything else.

So also in daylight will the Christian look at anything. He will cast his eyes around on this pleasure and that. But when the darkness gathers, his cry is, *"My God! my God! why hast thou forsaken me? O why art thou so far from helping me and from the words of my roaring?"* (Psalm 22:1).

THIRTEEN

ALL JOY AND PEACE

*Now the God of hope fill you with all joy
and peace in believing, that ye may abound in hope,
through the power of the Holy Spirit.*
—Romans 15:13

Alarge number of people profess to have believed in the Lord Jesus Christ, but they assert that they have no joy and peace as a consequence thereof. They do not make this profession by union with the Christian church or in any open manner, but when they are hard pushed on the matter of personal salvation, they will sometimes say, "I do believe in Christ, but still I am so unhappy. I am so miserable that I cannot believe I am saved." The statement is tantamount to this: the Word of God declares that whosoever believes in Jesus is not condemned, but they assert that they have believed in Jesus and, nevertheless, are haunted with fears of condemnation that lead them to believe that they cannot have been delivered from the wrath to come.

I speak to tender hearts and to those who desire to have tender hearts, to those who have their faces toward Jerusalem, though as yet they are traveling in the dark. If you are truly desirous to obtain joy and peace through believing, I trust that God may bless you in the obtaining of it.

Take care, while valuing joy and peace, that you do not overestimate them. Remember that joy and peace are, though eminently desirable, not infallible evidences of safety. There are many persons who have great joy and much peace who are not saved, for their joy springs from a mistake, and their peace is the false peace that does not rest upon the rock of divine truth but upon the sand of their own imaginations. It is certainly a good sign that spring has come when you find the weather to be so warm, but there are very mild days in winter. I must not therefore infer because the heat of the sun is at a certain degree, that therefore it is necessarily spring. On the other hand, we have cold days in spring that, if we had to judge by such evidences, might attest that we were in November rather than in May.

And so, joy and peace are like fine sunny days. They come to those who have no faith, who are in the winter of their unbelief. They may not visit you who have believed; or, if they come, they may not abide, for there may be cold weather in May, and there may be some sorrow and some distress of mind even to a truly believing soul.

Understand that you must not look upon the possession of joy and peace as being the absolute consequence of your being saved. A man may be in the lifeboat, but that lifeboat may be

TAKE CARE, WHILE VALUING JOY
AND PEACE, THAT YOU DO NOT
OVERESTIMATE THEM. REMEMBER
THAT JOY AND PEACE ARE,
THOUGH EMINENTLY DESIRABLE,
NOT INFALLIBLE EVIDENCES
OF SAFETY. THERE ARE MANY
PERSONS WHO HAVE GREAT JOY
AND MUCH PEACE WHO ARE
NOT SAVED, FOR THEIR JOY
SPRINGS FROM A MISTAKE,
AND THEIR PEACE IS THE FALSE
PEACE THAT DOES NOT REST
UPON THE ROCK OF DIVINE
TRUTH BUT UPON THE SAND OF
THEIR OWN IMAGINATIONS.

so tossed about that he may still feel himself exceedingly ill and think himself to be still in peril. It is not his sense of safety that makes him safe; he is safe because he is in the lifeboat, whether he is aware of this or not.

Understand then that joy and peace are not infallible or indispensable evidences of safety and that they certainly are not unchanging evidences. The brightest Christians sometimes lose their joy. Some of those who stand well in the things of God—and concerning whom you would entertain no doubt—entertain many suspicions, however, about themselves.

Joy and peace are the normal element of a Christian, but he is sometimes out of his element. Joy and peace are his usual state of being, but there are times when, with fightings within and wars without, his joy departs and his peace is broken. The leaves on the tree prove that the tree is alive, but the absence of leaves will not prove that the tree is dead. True joy and peace may be very satisfactory evidences, but the absence of joy and peace during certain seasons can often be accounted for by some other hypothesis than that of there being no faith within.

In the first place, to trust Christ because you just feel happy is irrational. Suppose a man would say during another monetary panic, "I feel sure that the bank my money is in is safe." Why? "Because I feel so easy about my money." Now anybody would say to him, "That is no reason." But suppose he said, "I feel sure that my money is safe," and you had asked, "What is the reason?" "Because I believe the bank is safe." "Oh," you say, "that is right enough; that is good reasoning." In the first case, he put the emotion in the place of the cause and tried to make that a cause, but that cannot be done.

If a man would say, "I have a large estate in India." You ask, "How do you know?" "Why, because I feel so happy in thinking about it." "You fool," you say, "that is no proof whatever, not the slightest." But if he says to you, "I feel very happy," and you ask him why, and he replies, "Because I have an estate in India." "Oh," you say, "that may be right enough." A man may be thankful for what he rightly possesses, but to make joy and peace the evidence of external facts is supremely ridiculous. For a man to say, "I know I am saved because I am happy," is most irrational, while to be happy because you are saved is right. Oh, I pray you, take care that you do not act so irrationally before God!

Consider another view. Suppose I was in fear about the health of some dear friend. "Well," I say, "I would like to have my friend healthy, but I want to feel safe about that friend. I do not know anything about the state of my friend just now, and I am uneasy. Now I tell you, if I could get to feel easy, then I would be convinced that my friend is well." "Why," you would justly reply, "there is no connection between the two things! The proper mode of procedure is to find out whether your friend is well, and then you will feel easy."

You say, "I would believe I am saved if I felt happy." Is there any logic in that? On the contrary! First, believe that you are saved, and then happiness will follow. You cannot believe that you are saved while you persist in doing what God does not tell you to do, namely, looking to your own joy and peace instead of looking to the finished work of Jesus Christ.

Christian men are but men. They may have a bad liver or an attack of bile or some other trial, and then they get depressed about it. I would defy the apostle Paul himself to help it. But what then? Well, then you can get joy and peace through believing.

I am the subject of depressions of spirit so fearful that I hope none of you ever gets to such extremes of wretchedness as I go to. But I always get back again by this: I know I trust Christ. I have no reliance but in Him. If He falls, I will fall with Him; but if He does not, I will not. Because He lives, I will live also, and I spring to my feet again and fight with my depression and my downcast soul and get the victory over them. So may you do, and so you must, for there is no other way of escaping from it. In your most depressed seasons, you are to get joy and peace through believing.

"Ah," says someone, "but suppose you have fallen into some great sin—what then?" Why then all the more reason that you should cast yourself upon Him. Do you think Jesus Christ is only for little sinners? Is He a doctor that only heals headaches? It requires no faith to trust Christ when I do not have any sin, but it is true faith when I am foul, black, and filthy. When during the day I have tripped up and fallen, doing serious damage to my joy and peace, I go back by faith to that dear fountain and say, "Lord, I never loved washing so much before as I do tonight, for today I have made a fool of myself. I have said and done what I ought not to have done, and I am ashamed and full of confusion, but I believe Christ can save me, even me, and I will rest in Him still."

FOURTEEN

MR. READY-TO-HALT AND HIS COMPANIONS

God hath dealt to every man the measure of faith.
—Romans 12:3

When faith first commences in the soul, it is like a grain of mustard seed, which the Savior said was the least of all seeds. But as God the Holy Spirit is pleased to bedew it with the sacred moisture of His grace, it germinates and grows and begins to spread, until at last it becomes a great tree.

To use another figure, when faith commences in the soul, it is simply looking unto Jesus. Perhaps even then there are so many clouds of doubts and so much dimness of the eye that we have need for the light of the Spirit to shine upon the cross before we are able even so much as to see it.

When faith grows a little, it rises from looking to Christ to coming to Christ. The person who once stood afar off and looked to the cross eventually plucks up courage, and finding heart, runs up to the cross. Perhaps he does not run but has to be drawn before he can so much as creep there, and even then it is with a limping gait that he draws near to Christ the Savior.

But that done, faith goes a little farther: it lays hold of Christ. It begins to see Him in His excellency and appropriates Him in some degree, conceives Him to be the real Christ and the real Savior and is convinced of His suitability. When it has done as much as that, it goes further: it leans on Christ, its Beloved. It casts all the burden of its cares, sorrows, and griefs upon that blessed shoulder and permits all its sins to be swallowed up in the great red sea of the Savior's blood.

Faith can go further still. Having seen and run toward Him, having laid hold of Him and leaned on Him, faith can next put in a humble, but sure and certain, claim to all that Christ is and all that He has done. Then, trusting alone in this, appropriating all this to itself, faith mounts to full assurance. Outside of heaven there is no state more rapturous and blessed.

But this faith is very small, and there are some Christians who never get out of little faith all the while they are here. You may have noticed in John Bunyan's *Pilgrim's Progress* how many Little-Faiths he mentions. There is our old friend Ready-to-Halt, who went all the way to the Celestial City on crutches, but left them when he went into the river Jordan. Then there is little Feeble-Mind, who carried his feeble mind with him all the way to the banks of the river and then left it. He ordered it to be buried in a dunghill so that none might inherit it. Then there is Mr. Fearing, who used to stumble over a straw and was always frightened if he saw a drop of rain, because he thought the floods of heaven were let loose upon him. You remember Mr. Despondency and Miss Much-Afraid, who were so long locked up in the dungeon of Giant Despair that they were almost starved to death, with little left of them but skin and bone. Poor Mr. Feeble-Mind, who had been taken into the cave of Giant Slay-Good, was about to be eaten by him when Great-Heart came to his deliverance.

John Bunyan was a very wise man. He has put a great many of those characters in his book because there are a great many of them. He has not left us with one Mr. Ready-to-Halt, but he has given us seven or eight graphic characters, because himself in his own time had been one of them and had known many others who had walked in the same path.

Little-Faith is quite as sure of heaven as Great-Faith. When Jesus Christ counts up His jewels at the last day, He will take to Himself the little pearls as well as the great ones. If a diamond is ever so small, still it is precious because it is a diamond. So it is with faith, be it ever so little, if it is true faith. Christ will never lose even the smallest jewel of His crown. Little-Faith is always sure of heaven, because the name of Little-Faith is in the book of eternal life. Little-Faith was chosen by God before the foundation of the world. Little-Faith was bought with the blood of Christ and cost as much as Great-Faith. *"For every man…half a shekel"* (Exodus 38:26) was the price of redemption. Every man, whether great or small, prince or peasant, had to redeem himself with half a shekel.

Christ has bought all, both little and great, with the same precious blood. Little-Faith is sure of heaven, for God has begun the good work in him, and He will carry it on. God loves him,

WHEN JESUS CHRIST COUNTS
UP HIS JEWELS AT THE LAST DAY,
HE WILL TAKE TO HIMSELF THE
LITTLE PEARLS AS WELL AS THE
GREAT ONES. IF A DIAMOND
IS EVER SO SMALL, STILL IT
IS PRECIOUS BECAUSE IT IS A
DIAMOND. SO IT IS WITH FAITH,
BE IT EVER SO LITTLE, IF IT IS
TRUE FAITH. CHRIST WILL NEVER
LOSE EVEN THE SMALLEST JEWEL
OF HIS CROWN.

and He will love him to the end. God has provided a crown for him and will not allow it to hang there without a head. He has erected for him a mansion in heaven, and He will not allow the mansion to stand empty forever.

Little-Faith is always safe, but he very seldom knows it. If you meet him, he is sometimes afraid of hell and very often afraid that the wrath of God abides on him. He will tell you that the country on the other side of the flood can never belong to a worm as base as he. Sometimes it is because he feels himself so unworthy, another time it is because the things of God are too good to be true, he says, or he cannot think they can be true for such a one as he. Sometimes he is afraid he is not one of the elect. Another time he fears that he has not been called right, that he has not come to Christ properly. Another time his fears are that he will not hold on to the end, that he will not be able to persevere. If you kill a thousand of his fears, he is sure to have another host by tomorrow, for unbelief is one of those things that you cannot destroy. "It hath," wrote Bunyan, "as many lives as a cat." You may kill it over and over again, but still it lives. It is one of those weeds that sleep in the soil even after it has been burned, and it only needs a little encouragement to grow again.

Now, Great-Faith is sure of heaven, and he knows it. He climbs Pisgah's top and surveys the landscape. He drinks in the mysteries of paradise even before he enters within the pearly gates. He sees the streets that are paved with gold. He beholds the walls of the city, the foundations of which are precious stones, He hears the mystic music of the glorified and begins to smell on earth the perfumes of heaven. But poor Little-Faith can scarcely look at the sun. He very seldom sees the light. He gropes in the valley, and while all is safe he always thinks himself unsafe.

Strong-Faith can well battle with the enemy. Satan comes along and says, *"All these things will I give thee, if thou wilt fall down and worship me"* (Matthew 4:9). "No," we say, "you cannot give us all these things, for they are ours already." "But," says the enemy, "you are poor, naked, and miserable." "Yes," say we to him, "but still these things are ours, and it is good for us to be poor, good for us to be without earthly goods, or else our Father would give them to us." "Oh," says Satan, "you deceive yourselves. You have no portion in these things. But if you will serve me, then I will make you rich and happy here." Strong-Faith says, "Serve you, you fiend? Away! Do you offer me silver? Behold, God gives me gold. Do you say to me, 'I will give you this if you disobey?' Fool that you are! I have wages a thousand times greater for my obedience than you offer for my disobedience."

But when Satan meets Little-Faith, he says to him, *"If thou be [a] son of God, cast thyself down"* (Matthew 4:6). Poor Little-Faith is so afraid that he is not a son of God that he is apt to cast himself down on the supposition. "There," says Satan, "I will give you all this if you will disobey." Little-Faith says, "I am not quite sure that I am a child of God, that I have a portion among those who are sanctified." He is very apt to fall into sin by reason of the littleness of his faith.

Yet at the same time, I must observe that I have seen some Little-Faiths who are far less apt to fall into sin than others. They are so cautious that they dare not put one foot before the other, because they fear they would step awry. They scarcely dare to open their lips, but they pray, "Lord, You open my lips," because they are afraid that they would let a wrong word out if they were to speak. Always alarmed lest they should fall into sin unconsciously, they have very tender consciences.

I like people of this sort. I have sometimes thought that Little-Faith clings more tightly to Christ than any other. A man who is very near drowning is sure to clutch the plank with the grasp of a drowning man, which tightens and becomes more clenched the more his hope is decreased. Little-Faith may be kept from falling, but this is the fruit of tender conscience and not of slight faith. Careful walking is not the result of limited faith. It may go with it, and so may keep Little-Faith from perishing. But small faith is in itself a dangerous thing, laying us open to innumerable temptations and taking away very much of our strength to resist them.

"The joy of the Lord is your strength" (Nehe-miah 8:10). If that joy ceases, you become weak and very apt to turn aside. Little-Faiths have many nights and few days; long winters and short summers; many howlings, but little of shouting; often playing upon the pipe in mourning, but very seldom sounding the trumpet in exultation.

Perhaps the only way in which most men have their faith increased is by great trouble. We don't grow strong in faith on sunshiny days. It is only in rough weather that a man gets faith. Faith is not an attainment that drops like the gentle dew from heaven; it generally comes in the whirlwind and the storm.

Look at the old oaks. How is it that they have become so deeply rooted in the earth? Ask the March winds, and they will tell you. It is not the April shower that did it, or the sweet May sunshine, but it was the rough wind of March, the blustering month of old Boreas, the Greek god of the north wind, shaking the tree back and forth and causing the roots to bind themselves around the rocks.

So must it be with us Christians. We don't make great soldiers in the barracks at home; they must be made amid flying shot and thundering cannon. We cannot expect to become good sailors on the Serpentine; they must be made far away on the deep sea, where the wild winds howl and the thunders roll like drums in the march of the God of armies. Storms and tempests are the things that make men tough and hardy mariners. They see the works of the Lord and His wonders in the deep. So it is with Christians. Great-Faith must have great trials. Mr. Great-Heart would never have been Mr. Great-Heart if he had not once been Mr. Great-Trouble. Valiant-for-Truth would never have put to flight those foes and been so valiant if the foes had not first attacked him. So it is with us; we must expect great trouble before we can attain to much faith.

FIFTEEN

JOY IN LIFE'S HARD TIMES

At evening time it shall be light.
—Zechariah 14:7

I will not notice the particular occasion when these words were uttered or try to discover the time to which they specifically refer. Rather, I will take the sentence as a rule of the kingdom, as one of the great laws of God's dispensation of grace, that *"at evening time it shall be light."* Whenever philosophers wish to establish a general law, they think it necessary to collect a considerable number of individual instances. Putting these together, they then formulate from them a general rule. Happily, this need not be done with regard to God. We have no need, when we look abroad in providence, to collect a great number of incidents and then from them generalize the truth. Since God is immutable, one act of His grace is enough to teach us the rule of His conduct.

Now, in one place I find it is recorded that, on a certain occasion during a certain adverse condition of a nation, God promised that at evening time it would be light. If I found that in any human writing, I would suppose that the thing might have occurred once, that a blessing was conferred in emergency on a certain occasion, but I could not extract a rule from it. But when I find this written in the Word of God—that on a certain occasion when it was evening time with His people, God was pleased to give them light—I feel myself more than justified in inducing from it the rule that to His people at evening time there will always be light.

The church at large has had many evening times. If I might choose a figure to describe her history from anything in this natural world, I would describe her as being like the sea. At times the abundance of grace has been gloriously manifest. Wave upon wave has triumphantly rolled in upon the land, covering the mire of sin and claiming the earth for the Lord of Hosts. So rapid has been its progress that its course could scarcely be obstructed by the rocks of sin and vice. Complete conquest seemed to be foretold by the continual spread of the truth. The happy church thought that the day of her ultimate triumph had certainly arrived, so potent was the Word delivered by her ministers, so glorious was the Lord in the midst of her armies, that nothing could stand against her. She was *"fair as the moon, clear as the sun, and terrible as an army with banners"* (Song of Solomon 6:10). Heresies and schisms were swept away. False gods and idols lost their thrones. God Almighty was in the midst of His church, and upon His white horse He *"went forth conquering and to conquer"* (Revelation 6:2).

Before long, however, it always has happened that there came an ebb tide. Again the stream of grace seemed to recede, as the poor church was driven back either by persecution or by internal decay. Instead of gaining upon man's corruption, it seemed as if man's corruption gained on her. Where once there had been righteousness like the waves of the sea, there was the black mud and mire of the filthiness of mankind. The church had to sing mournful tunes, when by the rivers of Babylon she sat down and wept, remembering her former glories and weeping over her present desolation.

So has it always been—progressing, retrograding, standing still a while, and then progressing once more and falling back again. The whole history of the church has been a history of onward marches and then quick retreats—a history that is, on the whole, a history of advance and growth, but which, read chapter by chapter, is a mixture of success and repulse, conquest and discouragement. So I think it will be, even to the last. We will have our sunrises, our meridian high point, and then the sinking in the west. We will have our sweet dawnings of better days, our Reformations, our Luthers, and our Calvins. We will have our bright noontide, when the Gospel is fully preached and the power of God is known. We will have our sunset of ecclesiastical weakness and decay. But just as sure as the eventide seems to be drawing over the church, *"at evening time it shall be light."*

We may expect to see darker evening times than ever before. Let us not imagine that our civilization will be more enduring than any other that has gone before it, unless the Lord preserves it. Perhaps the suggestion will be realized, which has often been laughed at as folly, namely, that one day men will sit on the

THE WHOLE HISTORY OF THE
CHURCH HAS BEEN A HISTORY
OF ONWARD MARCHES AND
THEN QUICK RETREATS—A
HISTORY THAT IS, ON THE
WHOLE, A HISTORY OF ADVANCE
AND GROWTH, BUT WHICH,
READ CHAPTER BY CHAPTER,
IS A MIXTURE OF SUCCESS
AND REPULSE, CONQUEST AND
DISCOURAGEMENT. BUT JUST AS
SURE AS THE EVENTIDE SEEMS TO
BE DRAWING OVER THE CHURCH,
*"AT EVENING TIME IT
SHALL BE LIGHT."*

broken arches of London Bridge and marvel at the civilization that has departed, just as men walk over the mounds of Nimrod and marvel at cities buried there. It is possible that all the civilization of this country may die out in blackest night. It may be that God will repeat the great story that has been so often told: "I looked, and lo, in the vision I saw a great and terrible beast, and it ruled the nations, but it passed away and was not." (See Daniel 7.)

But if ever such things would be and the world would ever have to return to barbarism and darkness, if instead of what we sometimes hope for—a constant progress to the brightest day— all our hopes would be blasted, let us rest quite satisfied that "*at evening time there shall be light,*" that the end of the world's history will be concluded in glory. However red with blood, however black with sin the world may yet be, she will one day be as pure and perfect as when she was created. The day will come when this poor planet will find herself unrobed of those swaddling bands of darkness that have kept her luster from breaking forth. God will yet cause His name to be known "*from the rising of the sun to the going down of the same*" (Psalm 113:3).

> And the shout of jubilee,
> Loud as mighty thunders roar,
> Or the fullness of the sea,
> When it breaks upon the shore,
> Shall yet be heard the wide world o'er.

We know that in nature the very same law that rules the atom also governs the starry orbs.

> The very law that molds a tear,
> And bids it trickle from its source,

That law preserves the earth a sphere,
And guides the planets in their course.

It is even so with the laws of grace. *"At evening time it shall be light"* to the church. *"At evening time it shall be light"* to every individual. Christian, let us descend to lowly things. You have had your bright days in temporal matters. You have sometimes been greatly blessed. You can remember the day when the calf was in the stall, when the olive yielded its fruit and the fig tree did not deny its harvest. You can recollect the years when the barn was almost bursting with corn and when the vat overflowed with oil. You remember when the stream of your life was deep and your ship floated softly on, without one disturbing billow of trouble to molest it. You said then, "I will see no sorrow. God has hedged me about. He has preserved me. He has kept me. I am the darling of His providence. I know that all things work together for my good, for I can see it is plainly so."

Well, after that, Christian, you have had a sunset. The sun, which had shone so brightly, began to cast his rays in a more oblique manner every moment, until at last the shadows were long because the sun was setting and the clouds began to gather. Though the light of God's countenance tinged those clouds with glory, yet it was waxing dark. Then troubles lowered over you: your family sickened, your wife died, your crops were meager, your daily income was diminished, your cupboard was empty, and you wondered for your daily bread. You did not know what would become of you.

Perhaps you were brought very low; the keel of your vessel grated upon the rocks; there was not enough of bounty to float your ship above the rocks of poverty. You used both industry and economy, and you added perseverance; but all was in vain. It was in vain that you rose up early, sat up late, and ate the bread of carefulness. You could do nothing to deliver yourself, for all attempts failed. You were ready to die in despair. You thought the night of your life had gathered with eternal blackness. You would not live always, but you would rather depart from this vale of tears.

Was it not light with you at evening time? The time of your extremity was just the moment of God's opportunity. When the tide had run out to its very farthest, then it began to turn. Your ebb had its flow; your winter had its summer; your sunset had its sunrise. At evening time it was light. All of a sudden by some strange work of God, as you thought then, you were completely delivered. He brought *"forth thy righteousness as the light, and thy judgment as the noonday"* (Psalm 37:6). The Lord appeared for you as in the days of old. He stretched out His hand from above. He drew you out of deep waters. He set you upon a rock and established your course.

SIXTEEN

CURE FOR HEARTACHE

Let not your heart be troubled,
neither let it be afraid.
—John 14:27

It is the easiest thing in the world in times of difficulty to let the heart be troubled. It is very natural for us to give up and drift with the stream, to feel that it is of no use "taking arms against [such] a sea of trouble," but that it is better to lie back passively and to say, "If one must be ruined, so be it."

Despairing idleness is easy enough, especially to evil, rebellious spirits who are willing to get into further mischief that they may have the wherewithal to blame God more, against whose providence they have quarreled. Our Lord will not have us be rebellious. He bids us to pluck up our hearts and be of good courage in the worst conditions.

Here is the wisdom of His advice, namely, that a troubled heart will not help us in our difficulties or out of them. It has never been perceived in time of drought that lamentations have brought showers of rain. Doubting, fears, and discouragement have never been observed to produce a thaw in seasons of frost. I have never heard of a man with a declining business who managed to multiply the number of his customers by unbelief in God. I do not remember reading of a person whose spouse or child was sick who discovered any miraculous healing power in rebellion against the Most High.

It is a dark night, but the darkness of your heart will not light a candle for you. It is a terrible tempest, but to quench the fires of comfort and open the doors to admit the howling winds into the chambers of your spirit will not stay the storm. No good comes out of fretful, petulant, unbelieving heart trouble. This lion yields no honey. If it would help you, you might reasonably sit down and weep until the tears had washed away your woe. If it were really to some practical benefit to be suspicious of God and distrustful of His providence, why then, you might have a shadow of excuse. But since this is a mine out of which no one ever dug any silver and an oyster bed from which a diver never brought up a pearl, we would say, "Renounce what cannot be of service to you; for as it can do no good, it is certain that it does much mischief."

A doubting, fretful spirit takes from us the joys we have. You do not have all you could wish, but you have much more than you deserve. Your circumstances are not what they might be, but still they are not even now so bad as the circumstances of some others. Your unbelief makes you forget that your health still remains if poverty oppresses you or that, if both health and abundance have departed, you are a child of God, and your name is not blotted out from the roll of the chosen.

There are flowers that bloom in winter, if we have the grace to see them. Never was there a night of the soul so dark but that some lone star of hope might be discerned, and never a spiritual tempest so tremendous but that there was a haven into which the soul could put if it only had enough confidence in God to head for it. Be assured that though you have fallen very low, you might have fallen lower if it were not that underneath you are the everlasting arms. A doubting, distrustful spirit will wither the few blossoms that remain on your bough. If half the wells are frozen by affliction, unbelief will freeze the other half by its despondency. You will gain no good, but you may get incalculable mischief by a troubled heart. This root bears no fruit except wormwood.

A troubled heart makes that which is bad worse. It magnifies, aggravates, caricatures, and misrepresents. If just an ordinary foe is in your way, a troubled heart makes him swell into a giant. "We were in their sight but as grasshoppers," said the ten spies who gave the evil report, "and we were as grasshoppers in our own sight when we saw them." (See Numbers 13:33.) But it was not so. No doubt the men were very tall, but they were not so big as to make an ordinary six-foot-tall man look as small as a grasshopper. Their fears made them grasshoppers by first making them fools.

If they had possessed ordinary, nominal courage, they would have been men; but being cowardly, they subsided into grasshoppers. After all, what is an extra three, four, or five feet of flesh to a man? Is not the bravest soul the tallest? If he is of shorter stature, but nimble and courageous, he will have the

There are flowers that bloom in winter, if we have the grace to see them. Never was there a night of the soul so dark but that some lone star of hope might be discerned, and never a spiritual tempest so tremendous but that there was a haven into which the soul could put if it only had enough confidence in God to head for it.

best of it. Little David made short work of great Goliath. Yet so it is. Unbelief makes our difficulties seem to be gigantic. Then it leads us to suppose that no soul had such difficulties before, and so we utter the self-centered cry, "*I am the man that hath seen affliction*" (Lamentations 3:1). We claim to be peers in the realm of misery, if not the emperors of the kingdom of grief.

Yet it is not so. Why? What ails you? The headache is excruciating! It is bad enough, but what would you say if you had seven such aches at once, with cold and nakedness along with them? Twitches of rheumatism are horrible—well can I endorse that statement! But, what then? Why, there have been men who have lived with such tortures all their lives, like Baxter, who could tell all his bones because each one had made itself heard by its own unusual pang. What is our complaint compared with the diseases of Calvin, the man who preached every daybreak to the students in the cathedral and worked on until long past midnight, all the while a mass of disease with a complicated agony? You are poor? Ah, yes! But you have your own room, scanty as it is, and there are hundreds on the streets who find sorry comfort there. It is true you have to work hard. Yes, but think of the Huguenot galley slave in times past, who for the love of Christ was bound with chains to the oar and scarcely knew rest day or night. Think of the sufferings of the martyrs of Smithfield or of the saints who rotted in their prisons. Above all, let your eye turn to the great Apostle and High Priest of your profession, and "*consider him that endured such contradiction of sinners against himself, lest ye be weary and faint in your minds*" (Hebrews 12:3).

His way was much rougher
And darker than mine,

Did Jesus thus suffer,
And shall I repine?

Yet, the habit of unbelief is to draw our picture in the blackest possible colors, to tell us that the road is unusually rough and utterly impassable, that the storm is such a tornado as never blew before, that our name will be written down in the wreck register, and that it is impossible that we will ever reach the haven.

Be of good cheer, soldier, the battle must soon end. That bloodstained banner, when it will wave so high; that shout of triumph, when it will trill from so many thousand lips; that grand assembly of heroes, all of them made more than conquerors; the sight of the King in His beauty, riding in the chariot of His triumph on streets paved with love for the daughters of Jerusalem; the acclamations of spirits glorified; and the shouts and songs of cherubim and seraphim—all these will make up for all the fighting of today:

And they who, with their Master,
Have conquered in the fight,
For ever and for ever
Are clad in robes of light.

SEVENTEEN

A WORD TO THE TROUBLED

Call upon me in the day of trouble:
I will deliver thee, and thou shalt glorify me.
—Psalm 50:15

Of all things in the world to be dreaded, despair is the chief. Let a man be abandoned to despair, and he is ready for all sorts of sins. When fear unnerves him, action is dangerous; but when despair has loosed his joints and paralyzed his conscience, the vultures hover around him waiting for their prey. As long as a man has hope for himself, you may have hope for him. But the devil's object is to drive out the last idea of hope from men, that then they may give themselves up to be his slaves forever.

Let me just say to those who are in trouble, which I hope every faithful Christian will repeat again and again: *There is hope.* There is hope about your financial difficulties, your

sickness, your present affliction. God can help you through it.
Do not sit down with your elbows on your knees and cry all day.
That will not get you through it. Call upon God who sent the
trouble. He has a great design in it. It may be that He has sent it
as a shepherd sends his black dog to fetch the wandering sheep
to him. It may be He has a design in making you lose temporal
things so that you may gain eternal things. Many a mother's
soul would not have been saved if it had not been for that dear
infant who was taken from her bosom. Not until it was taken
to the skies did God give the attracting influence that drew her
heart to pursue the path to heaven. Do not say there is no hope.
Others have been in as terrible a set of circumstances as you
have now. Even if it seems as if it has come to a crisis of bread,
yet still there is hope. Go and try again on Monday morning.
God's providence has a thousand ways of helping us if we have
the heart to pray.

Are you in despair about your character? It may be that
there is somewhere a woman who says, "I have fallen. My character is gone. There is no hope for me." My sister, there is lifting
up. Some who have fallen as terribly as you have slipped have
been restored by sovereign grace. There may be someone who
has been a drunkard or who is about to become a thief. No one
knows it, perhaps, but he is conscious of great degradation and
says, "I will never be able to look my fellowmen in the face." Ah,
my dear friend, you do not know what Christ can do for you if
you would only rest and trust in Him.

Suppose you could be made into a new creature—would not
that alter the matter? "Oh," say you, "but that can never be."
"Not true," I respond, "that will be." Christ said, *"Behold, I make
all things new"* (Revelation 21:5). *"If any man be in Christ, he is a*

Do not sit down with your
elbows on your knees and
cry all day. That will not get
you through it. Call upon
God who sent the trouble.
He has a great design in it.
It may be that He has sent it
as a shepherd sends his black
dog to fetch the wandering
sheep to him. It may be He has
a design in making you lose
temporal things so that you
may gain eternal things.

new creature" (2 Corinthians 5:17). There was an old fable about a spring at which old men washed their faces and grew young. Now there is a spring that welled up from the heart of the Lord Jesus. If an old sinner washes not only his face there, but also his whole spirit, he will become like a little child and will be clean even in the sight of God. There is still hope.

"Ah," says one, "but you do not know my case." No, my dear friend, and I do not particularly desire to know it, because this sweeping truth can meet it, whatever it is. *"All manner of sin and blasphemy shall be forgiven unto men"* (Matthew 12:31). *"The blood of Jesus Christ, his Son, cleanseth us from all sin"* (1 John 1:7). Noah's ark was not made to hold just a few mites, but the elephant, the lion, and the largest beasts of prey all entered and found room. So my Master, who is the great ark of salvation, did not come into this world to save only a few who are little sinners, but *"He is able also to save them to the uttermost that come unto God by Him"* (Hebrews 7:25). See Him over there, see Him on the cross in extreme agony, bearing griefs and torments numberless and sweating in agony, all for love of you who were His enemies. Trust Him. Trust Him, for there is hope and lifting up. However bowed down you may be, there is hope even for you in Jesus Christ.

I feel as if I were walking along a corridor, and I see a number of cells of the condemned. As I listen at the keyhole, I can hear those inside weeping in doleful, dolorous dirges. "There is no hope, no hope, no hope." I can see the warden at the other end, smiling calmly to himself, as he knows that none of the prisoners can come out as long as they say there is no hope. It is a sign that their manacles are not broken and that the bolts of their cells are not removed. Oh, if I could look in! I think I can. I think I can open the gate just a little and cry, "There is hope!"

The fiend who said there is no hope is a liar and a murderer from the beginning, and the father of lies (John 8:44). Yet, there is hope since Jesus died. There is hope anywhere except in the infernal lake. There is hope in the hospital when a man has sickened and is within the last hour before his departure. There is hope, though men have sinned themselves beyond the pale of society; hope for the convict, though he faces execution; hope for the man who has cast himself away. Jesus is still able to save.

"No hope" is not to be said by any member of the mariners' life brigade while he can sight the crew of the sinking vessel. "No hope" is not to be said by any one of the fire company while he knows there are living men in the burning pile. "No hope" is not to be said by any one of the valiant army of the Christian church while the soul is still within reach of mercy. "No hope" is a cry that no human tongue should utter, that no human heart should heed.

May God grant us grace whenever we get an opportunity to go and tell all we meet with who are bowed down, "There is lifting up." And likewise tell them where it is. Tell them it is only at the cross. Tell them it is through the precious blood. Tell them it is to be had for nothing, through simply trusting Christ. Tell them it is of free grace, that no merits of theirs are wanted, that no good things are they to bring, but that they may come just as they are and find lifting up in Christ.

Still, nothing will avail unless there is much prayer. We need to pray that God may give effectiveness to the counsels He has given us and reward our obedience with abundant fruit. Oh, beloved, prayer is the grandest thing for those of us who have no might of ourselves. It is wonderful what prayer can do for us.

A dear friend said the other day, "Look at Jacob. In the early part of his life there was much that was unseemly in his character, and very much that was unhappy in his circumstances. Crafty himself, he was often the victim of craft, reaping the fruit of his own ways. But one night in prayer— what a change it made in him! Why, it raised him from the deep poverty of a cunning supplanter to the noble peerage of a prince in Israel!" Bethel itself is hardly more memorable in Jacob's history than Peniel.

And what might one night spent in prayer do for some of us? Suppose we were to try it instead of the soft bed. We need not go to the brook. It is enough that, like Jacob, we were left alone in some place where sighs and cries would be heard by none but God. One night spent thus in solitary prayer might put the spurs on some of you and make you spiritual knights in God's army, able to do great exploits. Oh, yes! May all other gracious exercises be started in prayer, crowned with prayer, and perfected by much prayer.

EIGHTEEN

ALL THINGS WORK TOGETHER FOR GOOD

*For we know that all things work together
for good to them that love God, to them who are
the called according to his purpose.*
—Romans 8:28

We know that all things work." Look around, above, beneath, and all things work. They work, in opposition to idleness. The idle man who folds his arms or lies upon the bed of sloth is an exception to God's rule—for all things work except the lazy sluggard. There is not a star, though it seems to sleep in the deep blue firmament, which does not travel innumerable miles and work. There is not an ocean or a river that is not ever working, either clapping its thousand hands with storms or bearing on its bosom the freight of nations. There is not a silent nook within the deepest forest glade where work is not going on. Nothing is idle.

The world is a great machine, never standing still. Silently all through the watches of the night and through the hours of day, the earth revolves on its axis and works out its predestined course. Silently the forest grows, and eventually it is felled. All the while between its growing and felling, it is at work. Everywhere the earth works. Mountains work. Nature in its inmost bowels is at work. Even the center of the great heart of the world is ever beating. Sometimes we discover its working in the volcano and the earthquake, but even when most still, all things are ever working.

They are ever working, too, in opposition to play. Not only are they ceaselessly active, but they are active for a purpose. We are apt to think that the motion of the world and the different evolutions of the stars are like the turning of a child's windmill, producing nothing. That wise, old preacher Solomon once said as much as that:

> *The sun also ariseth, and the sun goeth down, and hasteth to his place where he arose. The wind goeth toward the south, and turneth about unto the north; it whirleth about continually, and the wind returneth again according to his circuits.* (Ecclesiastes 1:5–6)

But Solomon did not add that things are not what they seem. The world is not at play; it has an object in its wildest movement. Avalanche, hurricane, and earthquake are only order in an unusual form. Destruction and death are progress in veiled attire. Everything that is, and is done, works out some great end and purpose. The great machine of this world is not only in motion, but there is also something weaving in it, which as yet mortal eye has not fully seen, but which our text hints at when it says that it is working out for God's people.

All things work in opposition to Sabbath. We morally speak of work, especially on this day, as being the opposite of sacred rest and worship. At present, all things work. Since the day when Adam fell, all things have had to toil and labor. Before Adam's fall, the world kept high on a perpetual holiday, but now the world has come to its workdays and has to toil. When Adam was in the garden, the world had its Sabbath rest, but it will never have another Sabbath until the millennium dawns. Then, when all things have ceased to work and the kingdoms have been given to God the Father, the world will have her Sabbath rest. But at present, all things do work.

Let us not wonder if we have to work, too. When we have to toil, let us remember, this is the world's week of toil. The 6,000 years of continual labor, toil, and travail have happened not to us alone, but to the whole of God's great universe. The whole world is groaning and travailing. Let us not be backward in doing our work. If all things are working, let us work, too. "Work...*while it is day; the night cometh when no man can work*" (John 9:4). And let the idle and slothful remember that they are a great anomaly. They are blots in the great writings of God on work. They mean nothing. In the entire book of letters where God has written out the great word *work*, the idle are nothing at all. Still, let the man who works, though it be with the sweat of his brow and with aching hands, remember that, if he is seeking to bless the Lord's people, he is in sympathy with all things—not only in sympathy with their work, but in sympathy with their aims.

"All things work together." That is in opposition to their apparent conflicting. Looking upon the world with the mere eye of sense and reason, we say, "Yes, all things work, but they work contrary to one another. There are opposite currents. The wind blows to the north and to the south. The world's sailing vessel, it is true, is always tossed with waves, but these waves toss her first to the right and then to the left. They do not steadily bear her onward to her desired haven. It is true the world is always active, but it is with the activity of the battlefield, where hosts encounter hosts and the weaker are overcome."

Do not be deceived. It is not so. Things are not always what they seem. *"All things work together."* No opposition exists in God's providence. The raven of war is coworker with the dove of peace. The tempest does not strive with the peaceful calm; they are linked together and work together, although they seem to be in opposition. Look at English history. So many events have seemed to be conflicting in their day, but they have worked out for good! It might have been thought that the striving of barons and kings for mastery was likely to tread out the last spark of British liberty, but instead they kindled the pile. The various rebellions of nations, the heaving of society, the strife of anarchy, the tumults of war—all these things, overruled by God, have made the chariot of the church progress more mightily. They have not failed their predestined purpose, *"for good to them that love God, who are the called according to his purpose."*

I know it is very hard to believe this. "What?" you say, "I have been sick for such a long time. My wife and children, dependent on my daily labor, are crying for food. Will this work together for my good?" So says the Word, and so will you find it before long.

"I have been in the business world," says another, "This commercial pressure has brought me exceedingly low and distressed me. Is it for my good?" You are a Christian. I know you do not seriously ask the question, for you know the answer. He who said, *"All things work together,"* will soon prove to you that there is a harmony in the most discordant parts of your life. You will find, when your biography is written, that the black page harmonized with the bright one—that the dark and cloudy day only served as a glorious foil to set forth the brighter noontide of your joy.

"All things work together." There is never a clash in the world. Men think so, but it never is so. With much cleverness and art, the charioteers of the Roman circus might avoid each other's glowing wheels. But with skill infinitely consummate, God guides the fiery coursers of man's passion, yokes the storm, and bridles the tempest. Keeping each clear of the other, He still induces good, and even better than that, from seeming evil in infinite progression.

We must understand the word *together* also in another sense. *"All things work together for good."* That is to say, none of them work separately.

I remember an old minister using a very pithy and homely metaphor: "*'All things work together for good.'* But perhaps, any single one of those *'all things'* might destroy us if taken alone. For example, a physician prescribes some medicine for you. You go to the pharmacist, and he makes it up. There is something taken from this drawer, something from that vial, something from that shelf. Any one of those ingredients, it is very possible, could be a deadly poison and kill you outright if you would take it separately; but the pharmacist puts one into the mortar and then another and another. When he has ground them all up with his pestle and has made a compound, he gives them all to you as a whole, and together they work for your good. But any single one of the ingredients might either have operated fatally or in a manner detrimental to your health."

Learn, then, that it is wrong to ask, concerning any particular act of providence, if it is for your good. Remember, it is not the one thing alone that is for your good; it is the one thing put with another thing, and that with a third, and that with a fourth, and all these mixed together that work for your good. Your being sick very probably might not be for your good, except that God has something to follow your sickness, some blessed deliverance to follow your poverty. He knows that, when He has mixed the different experiences of your life together, they will produce good for your soul and eternal good for your spirit.

We know very well that there are many things that happen to us in our lives that would be the ruin of us if we were always to continue in the same condition. Too much joy would intoxicate us; too much misery would drive us to despair. But the joy and the misery, the battle and the victory, the storm and the calm, all these compounded make that sacred elixir by which God makes all His people perfect through suffering and leads them to ultimate happiness. "*All things work together for good.*"

There are different senses to the word *good*. There is the worldling's sense of the word by which he means transient good, the good of the moment. "Who will put honey into my mouth? Who will feed my belly with hidden treasures? Who will drape my back with purple and make my table groan with plenty?" That is "good" to the world—the vat bursting with wine, the barn full of corn! Now, God has never promised that all things

Too much joy would intoxicate us; too much misery would drive us to despair. But the joy and the misery, the battle and the victory, the storm and the calm, all these compounded make that sacred elixir by which God makes all His people perfect through suffering and leads them to ultimate happiness. *"All things work together for good."*

will work together for such good as that to His people. Very likely, all things will work together in a totally contrary way to that. Do not expect, Christian, that all things will work together to make you rich. It is just possible they may all work to make you poor. It may be that all the different providences that will happen to you will come wave upon wave, washing your fortune upon the rocks until it is wrecked. Then waves will break over you, until, in that poor boat of the humble remnant of your fortune, you will be out on the wide sea with none to help you but God Almighty. Do not expect, then, that all things will work together for your material good.

The Christian understands the word *good* in another sense. By good, he understands spiritual good. "Ah!" says he, "I do not call gold good, but I call faith good! I do not think it always for my good to increase in treasure, but I know it is good to grow in grace. I do not know that it is for my good that I should walk in the circles of high society, but I know that it is for my good that I walk humbly with my God.

"I do not know that it is necessarily for my good that my children should be about me, like olive branches around my table, but I know that it is for my good that I flourish in the courts of my God and that I become the means of winning souls from going down into the pit. I am not certain that it is altogether for my good to have kind, generous friends with whom I may have fellowship, but I know that it is for my good that I have fellowship with Christ, that I have communion with Him, even though it is in His sufferings. I know it is good for me that my faith, my love, my every grace grow and increase, and that I would be conformed to the image of Jesus Christ my blessed Lord and Master."

To a Christian, however, the highest good he can receive on earth is to grow in grace. "There!" he says, "I would rather be bankrupt in business than I would be bankrupt in grace. Let my fortune be decreased. Better that than that I would backslide! Let your waves and your billows roll over me. Better an ocean of trouble than a drop of sin. I would rather have your rod a thousand times upon my shoulders, O my God, than I would even once put out my hand to touch that which is forbidden or allow my foot to run in the way of gainsayers." The highest good a Christian has here on earth is spiritual.

All things work together for a Christian's lasting good. They all work to bring him to the Savior's feet. *"So He bringeth them unto their desired haven"* (Psalm 107:30), said the psalmist—by storm and tempest, flood and hurricane. All the waves of troubles in a Christian's life simply wash him nearer heaven's shores. The rough winds only hurry his passage across the straits of this life to the port of eternal peace. All things work together for the Christian's eternal and spiritual good.

Yet sometimes all things work together for the Christian's temporal good. You know the story of old Jacob. *"Joseph is not, Simeon is not, and now ye will take Benjamin away; all these things are against me"* (Genesis 42:36), said the old patriarch. However, if he could have read God's secrets, he might have found that Simeon was not lost, for he was retained as a hostage; that Joseph was not lost, but gone before to smooth the passage of his gray hairs into the grave; and that even Benjamin was to be taken away by Joseph in love for his brother. So what seemed to be against him, even in temporal matters, was for him.

You may have also heard the story of that eminent martyr who habitually said, *"All things work together for good."* When he was seized by the officers of Queen Mary to be taken to the stake to be burned, he was treated so roughly on the road that he broke his leg. The officers jeeringly said, "*All things work together for good,*' do they? How will your broken leg work for your good?" "I don't know how it will," said he, "but for my good I know it will work, and you will see it so." Strangely, it proved true that it was for his good. Having been delayed a day or so on the road through his lameness, he arrived in London just in time to hear that Elizabeth was proclaimed queen. So he escaped the stake by his broken leg. He turned to the men who had carried him—as they had thought—to his death and said to them, "Now will you believe that '*all things work together for good'?*"

Though the primary meaning of the text is spiritual good, yet sometimes there may be carried in the main current some rich and rare temporal benefits for God's children, as well as the richer spiritual blessings.

NINETEEN

AN EVER PRESENT HELP

Fear thou not; for I am with thee: be not dismayed;
for I am thy God.
—Isaiah 41:10

We sometimes speak and think very lightly of doubts and fears, but such is not God's estimate of them. Our heavenly Father considers them to be great evils, extremely mischievous to us and exceedingly dishonorable to Himself, for He very frequently forbids our fears and as often affords us the most potent remedies for them. *"Fear not"* is a frequent utterance of the divine mouth. *"I am with thee"* is the fervent, soul-cheering argument to support it.

Unless the Lord had judged our fears to be a great evil, He would not so often have forbidden them or have provided such a heavenly sedative for them. Martin Luther used to say that to comfort a despondent spirit is as difficult as raising the dead. However, we have a God who both raises the dead from their graves and His people from their despair. *"Though ye have lien among the pots, yet shall ye be as the wings of a dove covered with silver, and her feathers with yellow gold"* (Psalm 68:13). *"Weeping may endure for a night, but joy cometh in the morning"* (Psalm 30:5).

More or less, all believers need consolation at all times, because their lifestyle is a very unusual one. The walk of faith is one protracted miracle. The life, the conflict, the support, and the triumph of faith are all far above the vision of the eye of sense. The inner life is a world of mysteries. We see nothing beneath or before us, and yet we stand upon a rock and go from strength to strength. We march onward to what seems destruction, but we find safety blooming beneath our feet. During our whole Christian career, the promises of God must be applied to the heart, or else—such is the weakness of flesh and blood—we are ready to go back to the flesh pots of the Egypt of carnal senses and leave the delights that faith alone can yield us.

There are certain special occasions when the Comforter's work is needed. One of these certainly is when we are racked with physical pain. Many bodily pains can be borne without affecting the mind, but there are certain others whose sharp fangs insinuate themselves into the marrow of our nature, boring their way most horribly through the brain and the spirit. For these, much grace is needed. When the head is throbbing, the heart is palpitating, and the whole system is disarranged, it is natural to say with Jacob, *"All these things are against me,"* to complain of the lack of providence, and to think that we are

More or less, all believers need consolation at all times, because their lifestyle is a very unusual one. The walk of faith is one protracted miracle. The life, the conflict, the support, and the triumph of faith are all far above the vision of the eye of sense. The inner life is a world of mysteries. We see nothing beneath or before us, and yet we stand upon a rock and go from strength to strength.

the ones above all others who have seen affliction. Then is the time for the promise to be applied with power. *"Fear thou not; for I am with thee."* The Lord has promised to strengthen and sustain you when you are sick. (See Psalm 41:3.) When bodily pain gives every sign of increasing or we expect the dreadful surgeon's knife, then to be sustained under such sufferings—the mere thought of which brings shudders to the flesh—we want the upholding gentleness of God. Like the song of the nightingale, *"Fear thou not; for I am with thee"* is sweetest when heard in the night.

When the trouble comes in our relative sorrows, borne personally by those dear to us; when we see them fading gradually by consumption, like lilies snapped at the stalk; or when suddenly they are swept away as the flowers fall beneath the mower's scythe; when we have to visit the grave again and again, and each time leave a part of ourselves behind; when our garments are the banners of our woe, and we desire to sit down in the dust and sprinkle ashes upon our heads because the desire of our eyes is taken from us—then we require the heavenly Comforter. Then, indeed, skillful counsel is in great request, and sweet to the heart are words like these: *"Fear thou not; for I am with thee: be not dismayed; for I am thy God."*

When all the currents of providence run counter to us; when, after taking arms against a sea of trouble, we find ourselves unable to stem the boisterous torrent and are being swept down the stream, loss succeeding loss, riches taking to themselves wings and flying away until we see nothing before us but absolute want, and perhaps are brought actually to know what want is—then we require abundant grace to sustain our spirits. It is not so easy to come down from wealth to penury, from abundance to poverty, with perfect resignation. That is a philosophy to be learned only where Paul was taught it, when he said, *"I have learned, in whatsoever state I am, therewith to be content"* (Philippians 4:11).

Some would find it hard to be content in the widow's position, with seven children and nothing to maintain them but the shameful pittance that is wrung out by her for her labors with her needle, at which she sits, stitching far into the dead of the night, sewing her very soul away. You might not find it quite so easy to bear poverty if you were shunned by men who courted you in prosperity, but who now do not know you if they meet you in the street. There are bitter things about the poor man's lot that are not easily rinsed from his cup. Then it is that the gracious soul needs the promise, *"Fear thou not; for I am with thee"* (Isaiah 41:10). *"Thy Maker is thine husband"* (Isaiah 54:5). *"A father of the fatherless, and a judge of the widow is God in His holy habitation"* (Psalm 68:5). If you are brought into this condition, may my Lord and Master say to you, *"It is I, be not afraid"* (John 6:20).

Dear reader, did you ever stand, as a servant of God, alone in the midst of opposition? Were you ever called to attack some deadly popular error, and, with rough bold hand, like an iconoclast, to dash down the graven images of the age? Have you heard the clamor of many, some saying one thing and some the other—some saying, "He is a good man," but others saying, "No, he deceives the people"? Did you ever see the rancor of the priests of Baal flashing from their faces and foaming from their mouths? Did you ever read their hard expressions, see their misrepresentations of your speech and of your motives? Did you never feel the delight of saying, "The best of all is that God is with us; and, in the name of God, instead of folding up the standard, we will set up our banners. If this is vile, we purpose to be viler still and throw down the gauntlet once more in the name of the God of truth, against the error of the times"?

If you have ever passed through the ordeal, then you have needed the words, *"Fear thou not; for I am with thee: be not dismayed; for I am thy God"* (Isaiah 41:10). *"Who are thou, that thou shouldest be afraid of a man that shall die, and of the son of man which shall be made as grass?"* (Isaiah 51:12). *"I will make thee unto this people a fenced brazen wall: and they shall fight against thee, but they shall not prevail against thee"* (Jeremiah 15:20). *"Fear not: for thou shalt not be ashamed"* (Isaiah 54:4).

But, my dear reader, we will want this word of comfort most of all when we travel down the banks of the final black river, when we hear the booming of its waves, feel the chilling influence of its dark flood, but cannot see to the other side. When the mists of depression of spirit hide from us *"the heavenly Jerusalem"* (Hebrews 12:22), and our eye catches no glimpse of the *"land that floweth with milk and honey"* (Leviticus 20:24), then the soul is occupied with present pain and wrapped in darkness that may be felt. In such a condition:

> We linger shivering on the brink,
> And fear to launch away.

We talk of death too lightly. It is solemn work to the best of men. It would be no child's play to an apostle to die. Yet if we can hear the whisper, *"Fear thou not; for I am with thee,"* then the mists will sweep away from the river, and that stream, turbid though it was before, will become clear as crystal, and we will see the "Rock of Ages" at the bottom of the flood. Then will we descend with confidence, hear the splash of the death stream, and think it music. It will be music as it melts into the songs of the seraphim, who will accompany us through its depths.

And it will be delightful when those mists have rolled away to see the shining ones coming to meet us, to go with us up the celestial hills to the pearly gates, to accompany us to the throne of God, where we will rest forever. Happy are they who will hear their Lord say to them, "*I am with thee; be not afraid.*"

After death, we read in this word of great events, what will happen to us, but we only feebly comprehend the revelation. After death, solemnities will follow that may well strike a man with awe as he thinks upon them. There is a judgment and a resurrection. There is a trumpet that will summon the sons of men to hear from heaven's doomsday book their future destiny. The world will be on fire, and the elements will melt with fervent heat. The time will surely come when there will be a pompous appearing of the great Judge at the dread inquest. There will be the finalization of the dispensation and the gathering together of all things in one that are in Christ. There will be a casting down into hell of the tares bound up in bundles to burn, and the fire that will never be quenched will send up its smoke forever and ever.

What about that future? Why, faith can look forward to it without a single tremor. She does not fear, for she hears the voice of the everlasting God saying to her, "'*I am with thee.*' I will be with you when your dust rises. Your first transporting vision will be the King in His beauty. You will be satisfied when you wake up in His likeness. I will be with you when the heavens are ablaze, your Preserver, your Comforter, your Heaven, your All in All. Therefore, fear you not, but look forward with unmoved delight to all the mystery and the glory of the age unborn."

TWENTY

DELIVERANCE FROM SURROUNDING TROUBLES

Thou hast beset me behind and before,
and laid thine hand upon me.
—Psalm 139:5

No doubt the children of Israel supposed that all was over. The Egyptians had sent them away, entreating them to depart and loading them with riches. Terror had smitten the heart of Egypt. From the king on the throne to the prisoner in the dungeon, all was dismay and fear on account of Israel. Egypt was glad when they departed.

Thus, the children of Israel said to themselves, "We will now march to Canaan at once. There will be no more dangers, no more troubles, no more trials. The Egyptians themselves have sent us away, and they are too afraid of us ever to molest us again. Now we will tread the desert with quick footsteps. After a few days, we will enter into the land of our possession—the land that flows with milk and honey."

"Not quite so speedily," said God. "The time has not arrived yet for you to rest. It is true I have delivered you from Egypt, but there is much you have to learn before you will be prepared to dwell in Canaan. Therefore, I will lead you about, to instruct you and teach you." And it came to pass that the Lord led the children of Israel through the wilderness of the Red Sea, until they arrived over against Baalzephon, where the craggy mountains shut them in on either side. Pharaoh heard of it. He came upon them to overcome them. They stood in terrible fright and jeopardy of their lives.

Now, it is usually similar with a believer: he marches out of Egypt spiritually at the time of his conversion and says to himself, "Now I will always be happy." He has a bright eye and a light heart, for his fetters have been dashed to the ground. No longer does he feel the lash of conscience upon his shoulder. "Now," says he, "I may have a short life, but it will be a happy one."

A few more rolling years at most,
Will land me on fair Canaan's coast.

The Israelites had a great trial sent by God Himself. There was the Red Sea in front of them. Now, it was not an enemy who put the sea there; it was God Himself. We may therefore think that the Red Sea represents some great and trying providence, which the Lord will be sure to place in the path of every newborn child, in order to try his faith and to test the sincerity of his trust in God.

I do not know whether your experience will back up mine, but I can say this: the worst difficulty I ever met with, or I think I can ever meet with, happened a little time after my conversion to God. And you must generally expect, very soon after you have been brought to know and love Him, that you will have some great, broad, deep Red Sea straight before your path, which you will scarcely know how to pass.

Sometimes it will occur in the family. For instance, if he is an ungodly man, the husband may say, "You will not attend that place of worship. I positively forbid you to be baptized, or to join that church." There is a Red Sea before you. You have done nothing wrong. It is God Himself who places that Red Sea before your path. Or perhaps before that time, you were carrying on a business that now you cannot conscientiously continue. There is a Red Sea that you have to cross in renouncing your means of livelihood. You don't see how it is to be done, or how you will maintain yourself and provide things honestly in the sight of all men. Perhaps your employment calls you among men with whom you lived before on amicable terms, but now suddenly they say, "Come! Won't you do as you used to do?" The Red Sea before you is a hard struggle. You do not like to come out and say, "I cannot, I will not, for I am a Christian." You stand still, half afraid to go forward.

Perhaps the Red Sea is something proceeding more immediately from God. You find that just when He plants a vine in your heart, He blasts all the vines in your vineyard, and when He plants you in His own garden, then it is that He uproots all your comforts and your joys. Just when the Sun of Righteousness is rising upon you, your own little candle is blown out. Just when you seem to need it most, your gourd is withered, your prosperity departs, and your flood begins to ebb.

I say again, it may not be so with all of you, but I think that most of God's people have not long escaped the bondage of Egypt before they find some terrible, rolling sea lashed perhaps by tempestuous winds directly in their path. They stand aghast, and say, "O God, how can I bear this? I thought I could give up all for you, but now I feel as if I could do nothing! I thought I would be in heaven and all would be easy. But here is a sea I cannot ford. There is no squadron of ships to carry me across. It is not bridged even by Your mercy. I must swim it, or else I fear I must perish."

The children of Israel would not have cared about the Red Sea a single atom if they had not been terrified by the Egyptians who were behind them. These Egyptians, I think, may be interpreted by way of parable as the representatives of those sins that we thought were completely dead and gone. For a little while after conversion, sin does not trouble a Christian. He is very happy and cheerful, in a sense of pardon. But before many days are past, he will understand what Paul said, "*I find a law, so that when I would do good, evil is present with me*" (Romans 7:21). The first moment when he wins his liberty, the Christian laughs and leaps in an ecstasy of joy. He thinks, "Oh! I will soon be in heaven. As for sin, I can trample that beneath my feet!"

But, scarcely has another Sunday gladdened his spirit before he finds that sin is too much for him. The old corruptions, which he fancied were laid in their graves, resurrect and start up afresh. He begins to cry, "*O wretched man that I am! who shall deliver me from the body of this death?*" (Romans 7:24). He sees all his old sins galloping behind him like Pharaoh and his host pursuing him to the borders of the Red Sea.

There is a great trial before him. He thinks he could bear that. He thinks he could walk through the Red Sea. But those Egyptians are behind him! He thought he would never see them any more forever. They were the plague and torment of his life when they made him work in the brick kiln. He sees his old master, the very man who habitually laid the lash on his shoulders, riding hastily after him. There are the eyes of that black Pharaoh, flashing like fire in the distance. He sees the horrid scowling face of the tyrant, and how he trembles! Satan is after him, and all the legions of hell seem to be let loose, if possible, to destroy his soul utterly.

At such a time, moreover, our sins are more formidable to us than they were before they were forgiven because, when we were in Egypt, we never saw the Egyptians mounted on horses or in chariots. They only appeared as our taskmasters with their whips. But now these people see the Egyptians on horseback, clad in armor. They have come out with their warlike instruments to slay them.

These poor children of Israel had such faint hearts. They no sooner saw the Egyptians than they began to cry out. When they beheld the Red Sea before them, they murmured against their deliverer. A faint heart is the worst foe a Christian can have. While he keeps his faith firm, while the anchor is fixed deep in the rock, he never need fear the storm. But when the hand of faith is palsied, or the eye of faith is dim, it will go hard with us.

As for the Egyptian, he may throw his spear. While we can deflect it with our shield of faith, we are not terrified by the weapon; but if we lose our faith, the spear becomes a deadly dart. While we have faith, the Red Sea may flow before us, as deep and as dark as it pleases. Like Leviathan, we trust we can snuff up Jordan at a gulp. But if we have no faith, then at the most insignificant streamlet, which Faith could take up in her hands in a single moment and drink like Gideon's men, poor Unbelief stands quivering and crying, "Ah! I will be drowned in the floods, or I will be slain by the foe. There is no hope for me. I am driven to despair. It would have been better for me that I had died in Egypt than that I should come here to be slain by the hand of the enemy."

The child of God, when he is first born again, has very little faith, because he has had but little experience. He has not tried the promises and therefore he does not know their faithfulness. He has not used the arm of faith, and therefore the sinews of it have not become strong. Let him live a little longer and become confirmed in the faith, and he will not care for Red Seas or for the Egyptians. But just then his little heart beats against the walls of his body and he laments, "Ah, me! Ah, me! 'O wretched man that I am!' How will I ever find deliverance?"

Cheer up, then, heir of grace! What is your trial? Has providence brought it upon you? If so, unerring wisdom will deliver you from it. What is it with which you are now disciplined? As truly as you are alive, God will remove it. Do you think God's cloudy pillar would ever lead you to a place where God's right arm would fail you? Do you imagine that He would ever guide you into such a narrow ravine that He could not conduct you out again? The providence that apparently misleads will in truth befriend you. That which leads you into difficulties guards you against foes. It casts darkness on your sins while giving light to you.

How sweet is providence to a child of God when he can reflect upon it! He can look out into this world, and say, "However great my troubles are, they are not as great as my Father's power. However difficult my circumstances are, yet all things around me are working together for good. He who holds up the unpillared arch of the starry heavens can also support my soul without a single apparent prop. He who guides the stars in their well-ordered courses, even when they seem to move in mazelike dances, surely He can overrule my trials in such a way that out of confusion He will bring order and produce lasting good from seeming evil. He who bridles the storm and puts the bit in the mouth of the tempest, surely He can restrain my trial and keep my sorrows in subjection. I need not fear while the lightning is in His hands and the thunders sleep within His lips, while the oceans gurgle from His fist and the clouds are in the hollow of His hands, while the rivers are turned by His foot, and while He digs the channels of the sea. Surely He, whose might wings an angel, can furnish a worm with strength. He who guides a cherub will not be overcome by the trials of an ant like myself. He who makes the most ponderous orb roll in dignity and keeps its predestined orbit, can make a little atom like myself move in my proper course and conduct me as He pleases."

Christian, there is no sweeter pillow than providence! Even when providence seems adverse, believe it still, lay it under your head, because you may depend upon it that there is comfort in its bosom. There is hope for you, child of God! That great trouble that is to come in your way in the early part of your pilgrimage is planned by love, the same love that will interpose itself as your protector.

The children of Israel had another refuge. They knew that they were covenant people of God, and that, even though they were in difficulties, God had brought them there. Therefore, God (let me say it with reverence) was bound by His honor to bring them out of that trouble into which He had brought them. "Well," says the child of God, "I know I am in a predicament, but this is one thing I also know—I did not come out of Egypt by myself; I know that He brought me out. I know that I did not escape by my own power or slay my firstborn sins myself; I know that He did it. And though I fled from the tyrant, I know that He made my feet mighty for travel, for there was not one feeble in all our tribes. I know that though I am at the Red Sea, I did not run there uncalled, but He bade me go there. Therefore, I give to the winds my fears, for if He has led me here into this difficulty, He will lead me out and lead me through."

The third refuge that the children of Israel had was in a man. Neither of the two others, without him, would have been of any avail. It was the man Moses. He did everything for them. Your greatest refuge in all your trials, O child of God, is in a Man: not in Moses, but in Jesus; not in the servant, but in the Master. He is interceding for you, unseen and unheard by you, even as Moses did for the children of Israel. If you could, in the dim distance, catch the sweet syllables of His voice as they distill from His lips and see His heart as it speaks for you, you would take comfort, for God hears that Man when He pleads. He can overcome every difficulty. He has not a rod, but a cross, which can divide the Red Sea. He has not only a cloudy pillar

CHRISTIAN, THERE IS NO
SWEETER PILLOW THAN
PROVIDENCE! EVEN WHEN
PROVIDENCE SEEMS ADVERSE,
BELIEVE IT STILL, LAY IT UNDER
YOUR HEAD, BECAUSE YOU MAY
DEPEND UPON IT THAT THERE IS
COMFORT IN ITS BOSOM. THERE
IS HOPE FOR YOU, CHILD OF GOD!
THAT GREAT TROUBLE THAT IS
TO COME IN YOUR WAY IN THE
EARLY PART OF YOUR PILGRIMAGE
IS PLANNED BY LOVE, THE SAME
LOVE THAT WILL INTERPOSE
ITSELF AS YOUR PROTECTOR.

of forgiving grace, which can dim the eyes of your foes and can keep them at a distance, but He also has a cross that can open the Red Sea and drown your sins in the very midst.

Jesus will not leave you. Look! On yonder rock of heaven He stands, cross in hand, even as Moses did with his rod. Cry to Him, for with that uplifted cross He will cleave a path for you and guide you through the sea. He will make those old floods, which had been friends forever, stand asunder like foes. Call to Him, and He will make you a way in the midst of the ocean and a path through the pathless sea. Cry to Him, and there will not a sin of yours be left alive. He will sweep them all away. And the king of sin, the devil, he too will be overwhelmed beneath the Savior's blood, while you sing:

> Hell and my sins obstruct my path,
> But hell and sin are conquered foes;
> My Jesus nailed them to His cross,
> And sang the triumph as He rose.

TWENTY-ONE

A HARP'S SWEET NOTE

Fear thou not; for I am with thee.
—Isaiah 41:10

This harp sounds most sweetly. Saul was subject to fits of deep despondency. But when David, the skillful harpist, laid his hand among the obedient strings, the evil spirit departed, overcome by the subduing power of melody. Our text is such a harp, and if the Holy Spirit will but touch its strings, its sweet discourse will charm away the demon of despair. *"I am with thee."* It is a harp of ten strings, containing the full chords of consolation. Its notes quiver to the height of ecstasy or descend to the hollow bass of the deepest grief.

All through life, I may picture the saints as marching to its music, even as the children of Israel set out to the notes of the silver trumpets. Israel came to the Red Sea. They might well have been afraid because the Egyptians were behind them. The crack of their whips could be heard. The rolling sea was before them, but Israel marched confidently through its depths, because the word was given, "Fear not; the Lord God is with His people." See the pillar of cloud by day and the pillar of fire by night. How safely the Israelites followed their direction, even through the heart of the sea!

They trod the sand on the other side. It was an arid waste. How would they support themselves or their flocks? *"Fear thou not; for I am with thee."* Oh! The manna dropped from heaven, and the waters rippled from the rock. But, see, they came to Jordan! It was their last difficulty, and then they would reach the land of their inheritance. Jordan divided—what ailed you, O Jordan, that you were driven back? God was with His people. They feared not, but entered into their rest. This is the heritage of all the saints.

As I thought of the life of faith, I saw before my eyes, as in a vision, a lofty staircase of light. Led by an invisible hand, I mounted step by step. When I had ascended long and far, it turned again and again. I could see no supports to this elevated staircase, no pillars of iron, no props of stone. It seemed to hang in air. As I climbed, I looked up to see where the staircase went, but I saw no further than the step on which I stood, except that now and then the clouds of light above me parted asunder and I thought I saw the throne of the Eternal and the heaven of His glory. My next step seemed to be upon the air. Yet when I boldly put down my foot, I found it as firm as pavement beneath me. I looked back on the steps that I had trod and was amazed, but I dared not tarry, for "forward" was the voice that urged me on. I knew, for faith had told me, that the winding stair would end at last, beyond the sun and moon and stars in the excellent glory.

As now and then I gazed down into the depths out of which the stairs had lifted me, I shuddered at my fate, should I slip from my standing or should the next step plunge me into the abyss! Over the edge of the chasm where I stood, I gazed with awe, for I saw nothing but a gaping void of black darkness. Into this I must plunge my foot in the hope of finding another step beneath it. I would have been unable to advance, and would have sat down in utter despair, had I not heard the word from above of one in whom I trusted, saying, *"Fear thou not; for I am with thee."* I knew that my mysterious guide could not err. I felt that infinite faithfulness would not bid me take a step if it were not safe. Therefore, still mounting, I stand at this hour happy and rejoicing, though my faith be all above my own comprehension, and my work above my own ability.

We believe in the providence of God, but we do not believe half enough in it. Remember that Omnipotence has servants everywhere, set in their places at every point of the road. In the old days of the postal horses, there were always relays of swift horses ready to carry onward the king's mails. It is wonderful how God has His relays of providential agents; how, when He is finished with one, there is always another just ready to take his place. Sometimes you have found one friend who failed you. He just died and was buried. "Ah!" you say, "What will I do?" Well, well, God knows how to carry on the purposes of His providence. He will raise up another.

How strikingly punctual providence is! You and I make appointments and miss them by half-an-hour, but God never missed an appointment yet. God never is before His time—although we often wish He were—but He never is behind, not by one tick of the clock. When the children of Israel were to go down out of Egypt, all the Pharaohs in the pyramids, if they had risen to life again, could not have kept them in bondage another half-minute. *"Thus saith the LORD God of Israel, Let my people go!"* (Exodus 5:1). It was time, and go they must. All the kings of the earth, and all the princes thereof, are in subjection to the kingdom of God's providence. He can move them just as He pleases. As the showman pulls his string and moves his puppets, so can God move all that are on earth and the angels in heaven, according to His will and pleasure.

And now, trembler, why are you afraid? *"Fear thou not; for I am with thee."* All the mysterious arrangements of providence work for our good. Touch that string again, you who find yourselves in trouble, and see if there my harp is not a rare instrument.

God well knows how, if He does not interpose openly to deliver us in trouble, to infuse strength into our sinking hearts. *"There appeared an angel unto Him from heaven, strengthening Him"* (Luke 22:43), it is written of our Lord. I do not doubt but that invisible spirits are often sent by God from heaven to invigorate our spirits when they are ready to sink. Have you never felt it? You sat down an hour ago and wept as if your heart would break, and then you bowed your knee in solemn prayer and spread the case before the Lord. Afterward, when you came down from the chamber, you felt as if you could joyfully encounter the trouble. You were humbled and bowed down under it, as a child under a chastening rod, but you gave yourself up to it. You knew it was your Father that smote. So you did not rebel any longer, but went into the world determined to meet the

I DO NOT DOUBT BUT THAT
INVISIBLE SPIRITS ARE OFTEN
SENT BY GOD FROM HEAVEN TO
INVIGORATE OUR SPIRITS WHEN
THEY ARE READY TO SINK. HAVE
YOU NEVER FELT IT? YOU SAT
DOWN AN HOUR AGO AND WEPT
AS IF YOUR HEART WOULD BREAK,
AND THEN YOU BOWED YOUR
KNEE IN SOLEMN PRAYER
AND SPREAD THE CASE BEFORE
THE LORD. AFTERWARD,
WHEN YOU CAME DOWN FROM
THE CHAMBER, YOU FELT AS
IF YOU COULD JOYFULLY
ENCOUNTER THE TROUBLE.

difficulty that you thought would crush you, feeling that you were quite able to sustain it.

I have read of people who bathe in those baths of Germany that are impregnated with a lot of iron. After bathing, they have felt as if they were made of iron and were able, in the heat of the sun, to cast off the heat as though they were dressed in steel. Happy indeed are they who bathe in the bath of such a promise as this: *"I am with thee!"* Put your whole soul into that consoling element. Plunge into the promise, and you will feel your strength suddenly renewed, so that you can bear troubles that would have overburdened you before.

There is a way by which the Lord can be with His people, which is best of all, namely, by sensible manifestations of His presence, imparting joy and peace that surpass all understanding. I will not venture to explain the exhilaration and the rapture that is caused in a child of God by the consciousness that God is near him. In one sense, He is always near us. In another way, however, there is an opening of our eyes and an unsealing of our ears, a putting away of the external senses and an opening of the inner spiritual awareness by which the inner life of the Christian becomes wondrously conscious of the pervading presence of the Most High.

Describe it, I cannot, for it is not a thing for words. It is like what heaven must be, a stray gleam of the sunlight of paradise fallen upon this sinful world. You are as sure that God is with you as you are sure that you are in the body. Though the walls do not glow, the humble floor does not blaze with light, and no rustle of angels' wings can be heard, yet you are like Moses when he took his shoes from off his feet, for the place where you stand has become holy ground to you. Bowed down, I have felt it, until it seemed as if my spirit would be crushed. Yet at the same time, I felt lifted up until the exceeding weight of glory became so great a joy it was too overwhelming for flesh and blood.

Here is a person who has lost all his worldly goods and is very poor. He is met the next morning by a generous friend who says to him, "Fear not, you will go and share with me. You know that I am a person of considerable property. Fear not, I know your losses, but I am with you." Now, I feel sure that any person so approached would go home and say to himself, "Well, now, I have no need of any anxiety. I am rich, since one half of what my friend has is more than I had before." Yes, but may not the same losses that fell upon you fall upon your friend? May not the same reverses that have made you poor, make him poor? In that case, you are as poor as ever. Besides, your friend may change his mind. He may find you much too expensive a client, and he may shut his door against you one of these days. But, now, God says to you, "*I am with thee.*" Now, the Lord has much more than your friend. He is much more faithful. He will never grow weary of you. He cannot change His mind. Surely it is better for you to feel that God is with you than to rely upon an arm of flesh.

Is it not so? Believer, you will never prefer man to God, will you? Will you prefer to rest in a poor, changeable man's promise, rather than to rest upon the immutable covenant of God? You would not dare to say that, though I dare say you have acted as if you would. I am afraid, such is our unbelief, that sometimes we really prefer the poor arm of flesh to the almighty arm of God. What a disgrace to us!

But in our sober senses, we must confess that God's "*I am with thee,*" is better than the kindest assurance of the best of friends. You may be engaged in Christian service, working very hard. Would not you feel very happy if God were to raise up a dozen young spirits who would rally round and help? "Oh!" say you, "I could go then to my grave saying, '*Lord, now lettest You your servant depart in peace*' (Luke 2:29), since there are so many others enlisted in the good cause." Well, but is it so? Might they not also grow as weary as you have? And what are they compared with the world's needs? May they not soon be taken away or prove unfaithful? If God says, "*I am with thee,*" is that not better than twenty thousand of the brightest spirits and thousands of the most industrious missionaries? For what would they all be without God? So, the only comfort they can bring you, they have to borrow from Him first of all.

Take the naked promise of God, for it is enough, and more than enough, though all earth's springs were dry.

ABOUT THE AUTHOR

Charles Haddon Spurgeon was born on June 19, 1834 at Kelvedon, Essex, England, the firstborn of eight surviving children. His parents were committed Christians, and his father was a preacher. Spurgeon was converted in 1850 at the age of fifteen. He began to help the poor and to hand out tracts, and was known as "The Boy Preacher."

His next six years were eventful. He preached his first sermon at the age of sixteen. At age eighteen, he became the pastor of Waterbeach Baptist Chapel, preaching in a barn. Spurgeon preached over six hundred times before he reached the age of twenty. By 1854 he was well-known and was asked to become the pastor of New Park Street Chapel in London. In

1856, Spurgeon married Susannah Thompson; they had twin sons, both of whom later entered the ministry.

Spurgeon's compelling sermons and lively preaching style drew multitudes of people, and many came to Christ. Soon, the crowds had grown so large that they blocked the narrow streets near the church. Services eventually had to be held in rented halls, and he often preached to congregations of more than ten thousand. The Metropolitan Tabernacle was built in 1861 to accommodate the large numbers of people.

Spurgeon published over two thousand sermons, which were so popular that they literally sold by the ton. At one point his sermons sold twenty-five thousand copies every week. An 1870 edition of the English magazine *Vanity Fair* called him an "original and powerful preacher...honest, resolute, sincere; lively, entertaining." He appealed constantly to his hearers to move on in the Christian faith, to allow the Lord to minister to them individually, and to be used of God to win the lost to Christ. His sermons were scripturally inspiring and highlighted with flashes of spontaneous and delightful humor. The prime minister of England, members of the royal family, and Florence Nightingale, among others, went to hear him preach. Spurgeon preached to an estimated ten million people throughout his life. Not surprisingly, he is called the "Prince of Preachers."

In addition to his powerful preaching, Spurgeon founded and supported charitable outreaches, including educational institutions. His pastors' college, which is still in existence today, taught nearly nine hundred students in Spurgeon's time. He also founded the famous Stockwell Orphanage.

In his later years, Spurgeon often publicly disagreed with the emergence of modern biblical criticism that led the believer away from a total dependence on the Word of God.

Charles Spurgeon died at Mentone, France in 1892, leaving a legacy of writings to the believer who seeks to know the Lord Jesus more fully.

Welcome to Our House!

We Have a Special Gift for You ...

It is our privilege and pleasure to share in your love of Christian classics by publishing books that enrich your life and encourage your faith.

To show our appreciation, we invite you to sign up to receive a specially selected **Reader Appreciation Gift**, with our compliments. Just go to the Web address at the bottom of this page.

God bless you as you seek a deeper walk with Him!

WE HAVE A GIFT FOR YOU

whpub.me/classicthx

WHITAKER
HOUSE